Van and RV Camping at State Recreation Areas

Discover 656 Camping Areas at 415 Locations in 30 States

Published by:

Roundabout Publications
PO Box 569
LaCygne, KS 66040

Phone: 800-455-2207
Internet: www.RoundaboutPublications.com

Library of Congress Control Number: 2023937502

ISBN-10: 1-885464-88-6
ISBN-13: 978-1-885464-88-0

Table of Contents

Introduction

Huge portions of public lands, managed by a variety of government agencies, are available to the general public for recreational use. This book will guide you to 656 camping areas available from various State Agencies in 30 states.

You can learn more about these camping locations by visiting the state's park or tourism website. Please note that sites with tent camping only and areas accessible only by boat are not included in this guide.

Using This Guide

The guide is especially helpful when used along with Google Maps, Windows Maps, or a GPS device for locating and navigating to each camping area.

State Maps

A state map is provided to aid you in locating the camping areas. A grid overlay on each map is used when cross-referencing with each camping area.

Map Grid Chart & Alphabetical List

Following the state map is a chart showing the camping area ID number(s) located within a map grid. Following this chart is an alphabetical list of each camping area, which is especially helpful when you already know the name of an area. This list provides each location's ID number and map grid location.

Camping Area Details

Camping area details include information about each public camping area within the state. Preceding each location's name is the ID number and map grid location, which is used when referencing the state map.

Details for each camping area generally include the following information:

- Total number of sites or dispersed camping
- Number of RV sites
- Sites with electric hookups
- Full hookup sites, if available
- Water (central location or spigots at site)
- Showers
- RV dump station
- Toilets (flush, pit/vault, or none)
- Laundry facilities
- Camp store
- Maximum RV size limits (if any)
- Reservation information (accepted, not accepted, recommended or required)
- Generator use and hours (if limited)
- Operating season

- Camping fees charged
- Miscellaneous notes
- Length of stay limit
- Elevation in feet and meters
- Telephone number
- Nearby city or town
- GPS coordinates

The Ultimate Public Campground Project

Data for this publication is from The Ultimate Public Campground Project, which was established in 2008 to provide a consolidated and comprehensive source for public campgrounds of all types. Please note that despite our best efforts, there will always be errors to be found in the data. With over 45,000 records in our database, it is impossible to ensure that each one is always up-to-date.

Update: In 2022 The Ultimate Public Campground Project database was acquired by a GPS manufacture. As a result, updated information for this book will no longer be available - this is the last edition.

Happy Camping!

Common Abbreviations Used

CG	Campground
CR	County Road
MP	Milepost
TC	Trail Camp
TH	Trail head

Area Designations

OHV	Off-Highway Vehicle
PRL	Public Reserved Lands
RA	Recreation Area
SB	State Beach
SRA	State Recreation Area
SRS	State Recreation Site
SVRA	State Vehicular Recreation Area

Miscellaneous Agencies

DEC	Department of Conservation
DFWR	Department of Fish & Wildlife Resource
DNR	Department of Natural Resources
DPR	Department of Parks and Recreation
LENRD	Lower Elkhorn Natural Resources District
LLNRD	Lower Loup Natural Resources District
LPNNRD	Lower Platte North Natural Resource District
LPSNRD	Lower Platte South Natural Resource District
MDC	Missouri Department of Conservation
MNNRD	Middle Niobrara Natural Resources District
ND PRD	North Dakota Parks & Recreation Department
NNRD	Nemaha Natural Resources District
NWFWMD	Northwest Florida Water Management District
ODF	Oregon Department of Forestry
PHWD	Pat Harrison Waterway District

Alaska

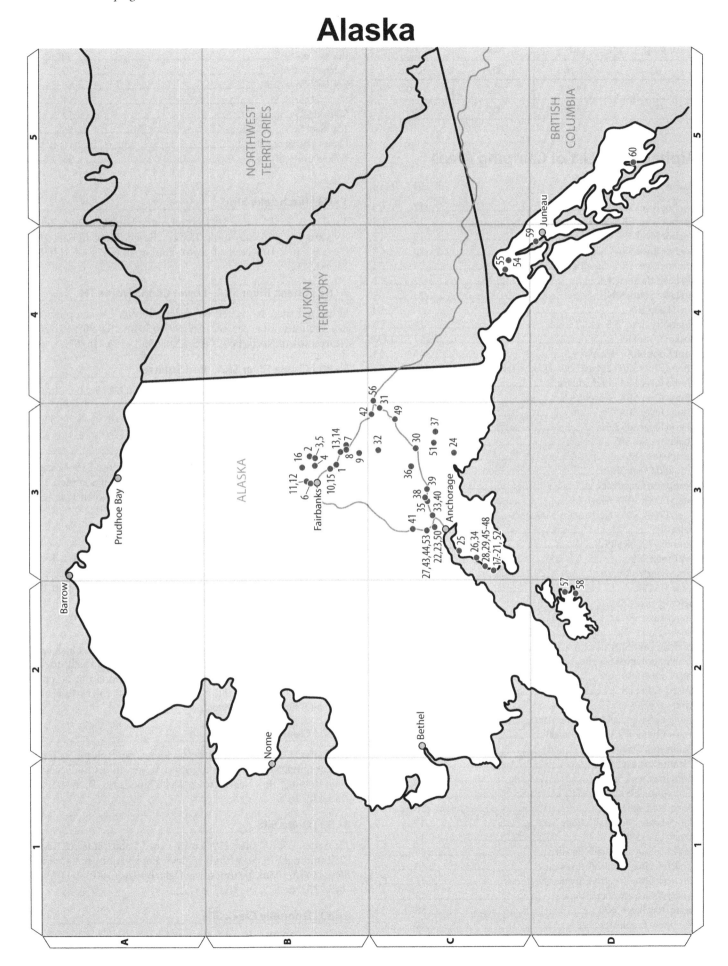

Map	ID	Map	ID
B3	1-16	D2	57-58
C3	17-53	D4	59
C4	54-56	D5	60

Alphabetical List of Camping Areas

1 • B3 | Birch Lake SRA

Total sites: 25, RV sites: 20, Central water, Vault/pit toilet, Tent & RV camping: $15, Stay limit: 15 days, Reservations not accepted, Elev: 825ft/251m, Nearest town: Fairbanks. GPS: 64.314699, -146.645432

2 • B3 | Chena River SRA - Lower Chena Dome TH

Dispersed sites, No water, No toilets, Tent & RV camping: $15, Reservations not accepted, Elev: 999ft/304m, Tel: 907-451-2695, Nearest town: North Pole. GPS: 65.034857, -146.216787

3 • B3 | Chena River SRA - Red Squirrel

Total sites: 5, RV sites: 5, Tent & RV camping: $15, Stay limit: 15 days, Reservations not accepted, Elev: 831ft/253m, Tel: 907-451-2695, Nearest town: North Pole. GPS: 64.935101, -146.283522

4 • B3 | Chena River SRA - Rosehip

Total sites: 37, RV sites: 37, Tent & RV camping: $15, Location approximate, Stay limit: 15 days, Reservations not accepted, Elev: 650ft/198m, Tel: 907-451-2695, Nearest town: North Pole. GPS: 64.879553, -146.753753

5 • B3 | Chena River SRA - Tors Trail

Total sites: 24, RV sites: 24, Central water, Vault/pit toilet, Tent & RV camping: $15, Stay limit: 15 days, Reservations not accepted, Elev: 745ft/227m, Tel: 907-451-2695, Nearest town: North Pole. GPS: 64.903862, -146.365264

6 • B3 | Chena River SRS

Total sites: 61, RV sites: 56, Elec sites: 11, Water at site, Flush toilet, No showers, RV dump, Tents: $20/RVs: $25-30, Also walk-to sites, Concessionaire, Stay limit: 15 days, Reservations not accepted, Elev: 445ft/136m, Tel: 907-452-7275, Nearest town: Fairbanks. GPS: 64.839837, -147.809612

7 • B3 | Clearwater SRS

Total sites: 17, RV sites: 17, Central water, Vault/pit toilet, Tent & RV camping: $15, Stay limit: 15 days, Reservations not accepted, Elev: 1046ft/319m, Nearest town: Delta Junction. GPS: 64.053223, -145.432726

8 • B3 | Delta SRS

Total sites: 25, RV sites: 25, Central water, Vault/pit toilet, Tent & RV camping: $15, Stay limit: 15 days, Reservations not accepted, Elev: 1141ft/348m, Nearest town: Delta Junction. GPS: 64.053266, -145.735736

9 • B3 | Donnelly Creek SRS

Total sites: 12, RV sites: 12, Central water, Vault/pit toilet, Tent &

RV camping: $15, Stay limit: 15 days, Elev: 1752ft/534m, Nearest town: Delta Junction. GPS: 63.698416, -145.891663

10 • B3 | Harding Lake SRA

Total sites: 105, RV sites: 100, Central water, Flush toilet, RV dump, Tent & RV camping: $15, 5 walk-to group sites, Stay limit: 15 days, Reservations not accepted, Elev: 734ft/224m, Nearest town: Fairbanks. GPS: 64.437739, -146.876056

11 • B3 | Lower Cahatanika SRA - Olnes Pond

Total sites: 15, RV sites: 15, Central water, Vault/pit toilet, No showers, No RV dump, Tent & RV camping: $15, Stay limit: 15 days, Reservations not accepted, Elev: 532ft/162m, Nearest town: Fairbanks. GPS: 65.077882, -147.744352

12 • B3 | Lower Chatanika SRA - Whitefish

Total sites: 25, RV sites: 25, Central water, Vault/pit toilet, No showers, No RV dump, Tent & RV camping: $15, Stay limit: 15 days, Open Jun-Sep, Reservations not accepted, Elev: 550ft/168m. GPS: 65.086049, -147.732906

13 • B3 | Quartz Lake SRA - Lost Lake

Total sites: 12, RV sites: 12, Central water, Vault/pit toilet, Tent & RV camping: $15, Stay limit: 15 days, Elev: 998ft/304m, Nearest town: Delta Junction. GPS: 64.197356, -145.838426

14 • B3 | Quartz Lake SRA - Quartz Lake

Total sites: 103, RV sites: 103, Central water, Vault/pit toilet, Tent & RV camping: $15, 87 RV spots in parking lot, Stay limit: 15 days, Elev: 1015ft/309m, Nearest town: Delta Junction. GPS: 64.197502, -145.828269

15 • B3 | Salcha River SRS

Total sites: 6, RV sites: 6, Central water, Vault/pit toilet, No showers, No RV dump, Tent & RV camping: $15, Stay limit: 15 days, Reservations not accepted, Elev: 654ft/199m, Tel: 907-451-2695, Nearest town: Fairbanks. GPS: 64.470866, -146.924527

16 • B3 | Upper Chatanika SRA

Total sites: 24, RV sites: 24, Central water, Vault/pit toilet, Tent & RV camping: $15, Stay limit: 15 days, Reservations not accepted, Elev: 1067ft/325m, Nearest town: Fairbanks. GPS: 65.231867, -146.883735

17 • C3 | Anchor River SRA - Coho

Total sites: 36, RV sites: 36, Central water, Vault/pit toilet, Tent & RV camping: $20, Stay limit: 14 days, Generator hours: 0600-2300, Reservations not accepted, Elev: 8ft/2m, Tel: 907-262-5581, Nearest town: Homer. GPS: 59.769744, -151.842527

18 • C3 | Anchor River SRA - Halibut

Total sites: 30, RV sites: 30, Central water, Vault/pit toilet, Tent & RV camping: $20, Stay limit: 14 days, Generator hours: 0600-2300, Reservations not accepted, Elev: 10ft/3m, Tel: 907-262-5581, Nearest town: Homer. GPS: 59.771944, -151.867036

19 • C3 | Anchor River SRA - Silver King

Total sites: 46, RV sites: 46, Central water, Vault/pit toilet, Tent & RV camping: $20, Stay limit: 14 days, Generator hours: 0600-2300, Reservations not accepted, Elev: 6ft/2m, Tel: 907-262-5581, Nearest town: Homer. GPS: 59.770879, -151.837806

20 • C3 | Anchor River SRA - Slidehole

Total sites: 30, RV sites: 30, Central water, Vault/pit toilet, Tent & RV camping: $20, Stay limit: 14 days, Generator hours: 0600-2300, Reservations not accepted, Elev: 26ft/8m, Tel: 907-262-5581, Nearest town: Homer. GPS: 59.770392, -151.854715

21 • C3 | Anchor River SRA - Steelhead

Total sites: 20, RV sites: 20, Central water, Vault/pit toilet, Tent & RV camping: $20, Stay limit: 14 days, Generator hours: 0600-2300, Reservations not accepted, Elev: 17ft/5m, Tel: 907-262-5581, Nearest town: Homer. GPS: 59.770291, -151.848477

22 • C3 | Big Lake North SRA

Total sites: 68, RV sites: 60, Central water, Vault/pit toilet, Tents: $20-25/RVs: $20-30, Also walk-to sites, Concessionaire, Stay limit: 7 days, Open Mar-Sep, Reservations accepted, Elev: 147ft/45m, Tel: 907-240-9797, Nearest town: Wasilla. GPS: 61.547087, -149.853934

23 • C3 | Big Lake South SRA

Total sites: 20, RV sites: 20, Central water, Vault/pit toilet, Tent & RV camping: $20-25, Concessionaire, Stay limit: 7 days, Reservations accepted, Elev: 146ft/45m, Tel: 907-240-9797, Nearest town: Wasilla. GPS: 61.532825, -149.831845

24 • C3 | Blueberry Lake SRS

Total sites: 25, RV sites: 25, Central water, Vault/pit toilet, No showers, No RV dump, Tent & RV camping: $20, Stay limit: 15 days, Open May-Sep, Reservations accepted, Elev: 2047ft/624m, Nearest town: Valdez. GPS: 61.120883, -145.700597

25 • C3 | Capt Cook SRA - Discovery

Total sites: 53, RV sites: 53, Central water, Vault/pit toilet, Tent & RV camping: $20, Stay limit: 14 days, Max Length: 40+ft, Reservations not accepted, Elev: 82ft/25m, Nearest town: Kenai. GPS: 60.805243, -151.015845

26 • C3 | Crooked Creek SRS

Total sites: 79, RV sites: 79, Central water, Vault/pit toilet, No showers, No RV dump, Tent & RV camping: $20, Stay limit: 7 days, Open May-Oct, Max Length: 35ft, Reservations not accepted, Elev: 49ft/15m, Tel: 907-262-5581, Nearest town: Soldotna. GPS: 60.321489, -151.286086

27 • C3 | Deception Creek SRS

Total sites: 7, RV sites: 7, No water, Vault/pit toilet, Tent & RV camping: Fee unk, Stay limit: 15 days, Reservations not accepted, Elev: 189ft/58m, Nearest town: Willow. GPS: 61.766211, -150.022199

28 • C3 | Deep Creek SRA - Beach CG

Total sites: 100, RV sites: 100, Central water, Vault/pit toilet, Tent & RV camping: $20, Stay limit: 15 days, Max Length: 35ft, Reservations not accepted, Elev: 10ft/3m, Tel: 907-262-5581, Nearest town: Homer. GPS: 60.029393, -151.703956

29 • C3 | Deep Creek SRA - North Scenic Overlook

Total sites: 29, RV sites: 29, Central water, Vault/pit toilet, No tents/RVs: $20, Stay limit: 15 days, Max Length: 35ft, Reservations not accepted, Elev: 28ft/9m, Tel: 907-262-5581, Nearest town: Homer. GPS: 60.030453, -151.681312

30 • C3 | Dry Creek SRS

Total sites: 50, RV sites: 50, Tent & RV camping: $20, Stay limit: 15 days, Reservations not accepted, Elev: 1559ft/475m, Nearest town: Glennallen. GPS: 62.153607, -145.475393

31 • C3 | Eagle Trail SRS

Total sites: 35, RV sites: 35, Central water, Vault/pit toilet, Tent & RV camping: $20, Stay limit: 15 days, Reservations not accepted, Elev: 1956ft/596m, Nearest town: Tok. GPS: 63.162329, -143.196029

32 • C3 | Fielding Lake SRS

Total sites: 17, RV sites: 17, No water, Vault/pit toilet, Tent & RV camping: $5, Stay limit: 15 days, Reservations not accepted, Elev: 2987ft/910m, Nearest town: Delta Junction. GPS: 63.193077, -145.647977

33 • C3 | Finger Lake SRA

Total sites: 24, RV sites: 24, Central water, Vault/pit toilet, Tent & RV camping: $25-35, Nothing larger than truck camper on waterfront sites, Stay limit: 7 days, Max Length: 35ft, Reservations accepted, Elev: 337ft/103m, Tel: 907-240-9797, Nearest town: Wasilla. GPS: 61.609952, -149.264364

34 • C3 | Johnson Lake SRA

Total sites: 51, RV sites: 51, Tent & RV camping: $20, Stay limit: 15 days, Max Length: 35ft, Reservations not accepted, Elev: 194ft/59m, Tel: 907-262-5581, Nearest town: Soldotna. GPS: 60.296483, -151.265256

35 • C3 | King Mountain SRS

Total sites: 22, RV sites: 22, Central water, Vault/pit toilet, Tent & RV camping: $25-30, Stay limit: 15 days, Reservations accepted, Elev: 803ft/245m, Nearest town: Chickaloon. GPS: 61.774985, -148.494753

36 • C3 | Lake Louise SRA

Total sites: 58, RV sites: 58, Central water, Vault/pit toilet, Tent & RV camping: $20, Concessionaire, Stay limit: 14 days, Reservations accepted, Elev: 2447ft/746m, Tel: 907-441-7575, Nearest town: Glennallen. GPS: 62.277745, -146.547663

37 • C3 | Liberty Falls SRS

Total sites: 10, RV sites: 10, Central water, Vault/pit toilet, Tent & RV camping: $25, 8 ton limit, Concessionaire, Stay limit: 15 days, Reservations not accepted, Elev: 1158ft/353m. GPS: 61.621603, -144.547945

38 • C3 | Long Lake SRS

Total sites: 9, RV sites: 9, No water, Vault/pit toilet, Tent & RV camping: Free, Stay limit: 15 days, Reservations not accepted, Elev: 1503ft/458m, Nearest town: Chickaloon. GPS: 61.804114, -148.236818

39 • C3 | Matanuska Glacier SRS

Total sites: 9, RV sites: 5, Central water, Vault/pit toilet, Tent & RV camping: $20, Concessionaire, Stay limit: 14 days, Max Length: 30ft, Reservations not accepted, Elev: 1675ft/511m. GPS: 61.800347, -147.815804

40 • C3 | Matanuska Lakes SRA

Total sites: 6, RV sites: 6, Central water, Vault/pit toilet, Tent & RV camping: $25, Concessionaire, Stay limit: 7 days, Reservations not accepted, Elev: 95ft/29m, Tel: 907-240-9797. GPS: 61.553208, -149.226388

41 • C3 | Montana Creek SRS

Total sites: 36, RV sites: 36, Central water, Vault/pit toilet, Tent & RV camping: $20, Concessionaire, Reservations not accepted, Elev: 254ft/77m, Tel: 907-733-8255. GPS: 62.103633, -150.059212

42 • C3 | Moon Lake SRS

Total sites: 15, RV sites: 15, Central water, Vault/pit toilet, Tent & RV camping: $20, Stay limit: 15 days, Elev: 1576ft/480m, Tel: 907-505-0319, Nearest town: Tok. GPS: 63.375453, -143.550878

43 • C3 | Nancy Lake SRA - South Rolly Lake

Total sites: 98, RV sites: 98, Central water, Vault/pit toilet, Tent & RV camping: $20-25, Stay limit: 14 days, Reservations not accepted, Elev: 204ft/62m, Nearest town: Wasilla. GPS: 61.666451, -150.137232

44 • C3 | Nancy Lake SRS

Total sites: 30, RV sites: 30, Central water, Vault/pit toilet, Tent & RV camping: $20, Near RR, Stay limit: 14 days, Reservations not accepted, Elev: 266ft/81m, Nearest town: Wasilla. GPS: 61.702368, -150.005312

45 • C3 | Ninilchik SRA - Ninilchik Beach

Dispersed sites, Tent & RV camping: $20, Stay limit: 15 days, Generator hours: 0600-2300, Reservations not accepted, Elev: 44ft/13m, Tel: 907-262-5581, Nearest town: Soldotna. GPS: 60.047932, -151.672954

46 • C3 | Ninilchik SRA - Ninilchik River

Total sites: 39, RV sites: 39, Central water, Vault/pit toilet, No showers, No RV dump, Tent & RV camping: $20, Stay limit: 15 days, Generator hours: 0600-2300, Max Length: 35ft, Reservations not accepted, Elev: 162ft/49m, Tel: 907-262-5581, Nearest town: Soldotna. GPS: 60.052526, -151.650734

47 • C3 | Ninilchik SRA - Ninilchik Scenic Overlook

Total sites: 9, RV sites: 9, No water, Vault/pit toilet, No tents/RVs: $20, Stay limit: 15 days, Generator hours: 0600-2300, Max Length: 35ft, Reservations not accepted, Elev: 98ft/30m, Tel: 907-262-5581, Nearest town: Soldotna. GPS: 60.048526, -151.653434

48 • C3 | Ninilchik SRA - Ninilchik View

Total sites: 14, RV sites: 9, Tent & RV camping: $20, Stay limit: 15 days, Generator hours: 0600-2300, Reservations not accepted, Elev: 51ft/16m, Tel: 907-262-5581, Nearest town: Soldotna. GPS: 60.046686, -151.670888

49 • C3 | Porcupine Creek SRS

Total sites: 12, RV sites: 12, Central water, Vault/pit toilet, No showers, No RV dump, Tent & RV camping: $25, Concessionaire, Stay limit: 3 days, Reservations not accepted, Elev: 2242ft/683m, Tel: 907-822-3973, Nearest town: Slana. GPS: 62.727782, -143.871425

50 • C3 | Rocky Lake SRS

Total sites: 11, RV sites: 11, Central water, Vault/pit toilet, Tent & RV camping: $20-25, Concessionaire, Stay limit: 7 days, Max Length: 32ft, Reservations accepted, Elev: 155ft/47m, Tel: 907-240-9797, Nearest town: Wasilla. GPS: 61.557652, -149.821246

51 • C3 | Squirrel Creek SRS

Total sites: 25, RV sites: 25, Central water, Vault/pit toilet, No showers, No RV dump, Tent & RV camping: $25, Stay limit: 15 days, Reservations not accepted, Elev: 1518ft/463m, Nearest town: Glennallen. GPS: 61.666563, -145.175452

52 • C3 | Stariski SRS

Total sites: 9, RV sites: 9, Tent & RV camping: $20, Generator hours: 0600-2300, Elev: 184ft/56m, Tel: 907-262-5581, Nearest town: Homer. GPS: 59.843207, -151.812229

53 • C3 | Willow Creek SRA

Total sites: 140, RV sites: 140, Central water, Vault/pit toilet, Tent & RV camping: $15, Stay limit: 4-15 days, Reservations not accepted, Elev: 107ft/33m, Nearest town: Willow. GPS: 61.773211, -150.162345

54 • C4 | Chilkoot Lake SRS

Total sites: 32, RV sites: 32, Central water, Vault/pit toilet, Tent & RV camping: $20, Stay limit: 15 days, Open May-Sep, Max Length: 35ft, Reservations not accepted, Elev: 102ft/31m, Nearest town: Haines. GPS: 59.335378, -135.565928

55 • C4 | Mosquito Lake SRS

Total sites: 5, RV sites: 5, Central water, No toilets, Tent & RV camping: Fee unk, Max Length: 20ft, Reservations not accepted, Elev: 273ft/83m, Nearest town: Haines. GPS: 59.453727, -136.022052

56 • C4 | Tok River SRS

Total sites: 43, RV sites: 43, Central water, Vault/pit toilet, Tent & RV camping: $20, Stay limit: 15 days, Max Length: 60ft, Reservations not accepted, Elev: 1649ft/503m, Nearest town: Tok. GPS: 63.325225, -142.831606

57 • D2 | Buskin River SRS

Total sites: 16, RV sites: 16, Central water, Vault/pit toilet, Tent & RV camping: $15, Stay limit: 14 days, Reservations not accepted, Elev: 60ft/18m, Nearest town: Kodiak. GPS: 57.756564, -152.496735

58 • D2 | Pasagshak River SRA

Total sites: 12, RV sites: 6, Central water, Vault/pit toilet, Tent & RV camping: $15, Stay limit: 7 days, Reservations not accepted, Elev: 66ft/20m, Nearest town: Chiniak. GPS: 57.465866, -152.456669

59 • D4 | Eagle Beach SRA

Total sites: 26, RV sites: 16, Central water, Vault/pit toilet, Tent & RV camping: $20, Stay limit: 7 days, Max Length: 35ft, Reservations not accepted, Elev: 47ft/14m, Nearest town: Juneau. GPS: 58.523576, -134.809002

60 • D5 | Settler's Cove SRA

Dispersed sites, Central water, Vault/pit toilet, Tent & RV camping: $15, Stay limit: 7 days, Max Length: 35ft, Reservations not accepted, Elev: 130ft/40m, Nearest town: Ketchikan. GPS: 55.510131, -131.724744

Arizona

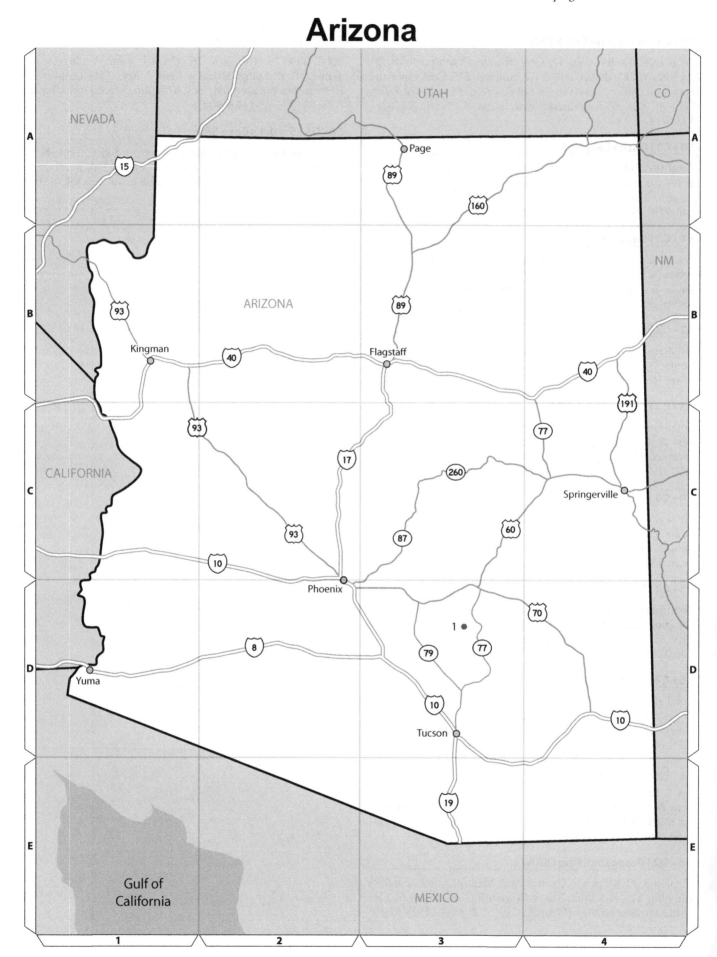

Map	ID	Map	ID
D3	1		

Alphabetical List of Camping Areas

Name	ID	Map
Mescal Mountain OHV Area	1	D3

1 • D3 | Mescal Mountain OHV Area

Dispersed sites, No water, No toilets, Tent & RV camping: Free, Elev: 2074ft/632m, Nearest town: Kearny. GPS: 33.062317, -110.896191

California

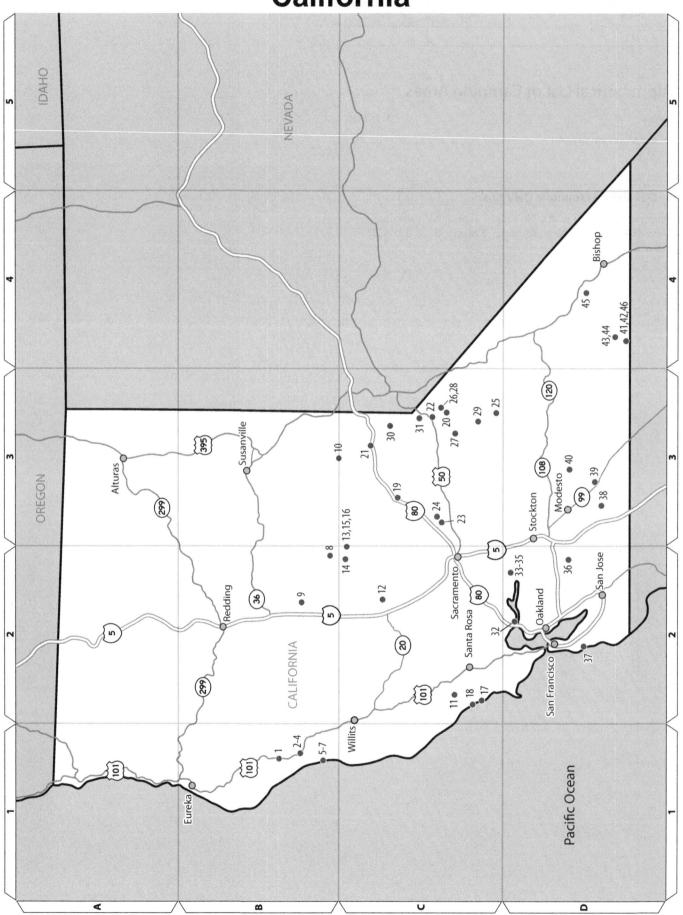

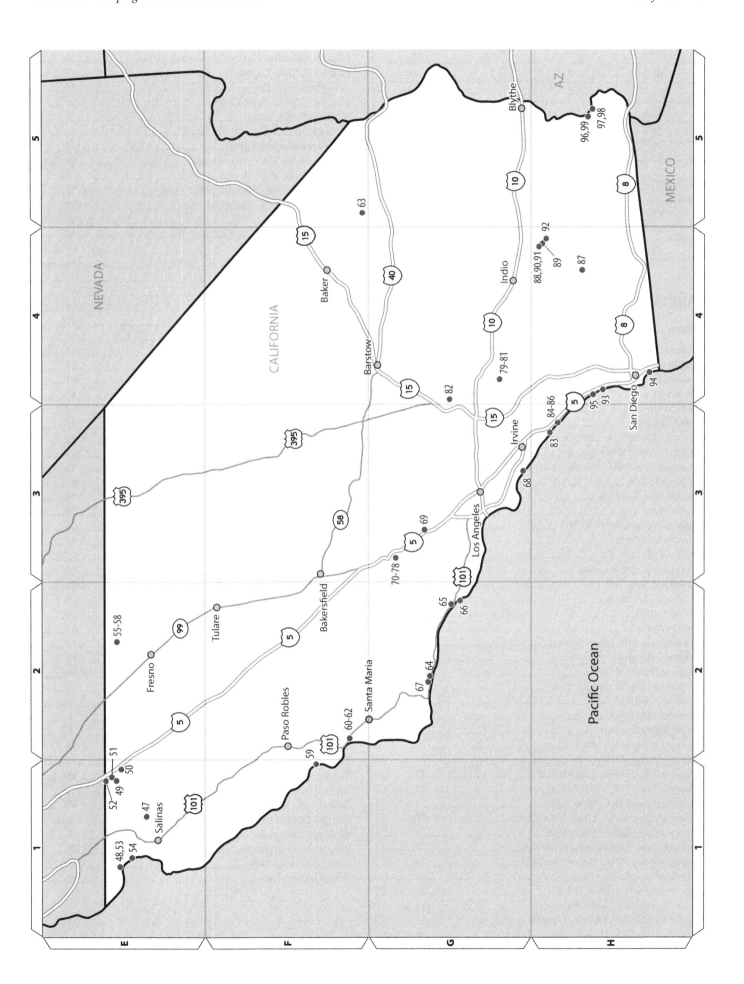

Map	ID	Map	ID
B1	1-7	F1	59
B2	8-9	F2	60-62
B3	10	F5	63
C2	11-18	G2	64-67
C3	19-31	G3	68-78
D2	32-37	G4	79-82
D3	38-40	H3	83-86
D4	41-46	H4	87-95
E1	47-54	H5	96-99
E2	55-58		

Alphabetical List of Camping Areas

1 • B1 | Benbow Lake SRA

Total sites: 75, RV sites: 75, Central water, Flush toilet, Free showers, RV dump, Tents: $35/RVs: $35-45, Open May-Sep, Max Length: 30ft, Reservations accepted, Elev: 440ft/134m, Tel: 707-923-3238, Nearest town: Garberville. GPS: 40.059991, -123.783004

2 • B1 | Standish-Hickey SRA - Hickey

Total sites: 62, RV sites: 62, Central water, Flush toilet, Free showers, No RV dump, Tent & RV camping: $35, Bike-in $5, Open all year, Max Length: RV-27, Trlr-24ft, Reservations accepted, Elev: 948ft/289m, Tel: 707-925-6482, Nearest town: Leggett. GPS: 39.876451, -123.730915

3 • B1 | Standish-Hickey SRA - Redwood

Total sites: 63, RV sites: 63, Central water, Flush toilet, Free showers, No RV dump, Tent & RV camping: $40, Open all year, Max Length: RV-27, Trlr-24ft, Reservations accepted, Elev: 735ft/224m, Tel: 707-925-6482, Nearest town: Leggett. GPS: 39.873864, -123.726557

4 • B1 | Standish-Hickey SRA - Rock Creek

Total sites: 35, RV sites: 35, Central water, Flush toilet, Free showers, No RV dump, Tent & RV camping: $35, Bike-in $5, Open all year, Max Length: RV-27, Trlr-24ft, Reservations accepted, Elev: 938ft/286m, Tel: 707-925-6482, Nearest town: Leggett. GPS: 39.876997, -123.724847

5 • B1 | Westport-Union Landing SB - DeHaven

Total sites: 41, RV sites: 41, No water, Vault/pit toilet, No showers, No RV dump, Tent & RV camping: $35, Reservations not accepted, Elev: 80ft/24m, Tel: 707-964-4406, Nearest town: Westport. GPS: 39.668179, -123.790467

6 • B1 | Westport-Union Landing SB - Howard Creek North

Total sites: 31, RV sites: 31, No water, Vault/pit toilet, No showers, No RV dump, Tent & RV camping: $35, Reservations not accepted, Elev: 59ft/18m, Tel: 707-964-4406, Nearest town: Westport. GPS: 39.679372, -123.790885

7 • B1 | Westport-Union Landing SB - Howard Creek South

Total sites: 13, RV sites: 13, No water, Vault/pit toilet, No showers, No RV dump, Tent & RV camping: $35, Reservations not accepted, Elev: 62ft/19m, Tel: 707-964-4406, Nearest town: Westport. GPS: 39.675374, -123.790725

8 • B2 | Lake Oroville SRA - Lime Saddle

Total sites: 44, RV sites: 44, Central water, No toilets, No showers, RV dump, Tents: $25/RVs: $45, Reservations accepted, Elev: 1010ft/308m, Tel: 530-876-8516, Nearest town: Oroville. GPS: 39.681504, -121.558074

9 • B2 | Woodson Bridge SRA

Total sites: 37, RV sites: 37, Central water, Flush toilet, Free showers, Tent & RV camping: $31, Group site $165, Open all year, Max Length: 31ft, Reservations accepted, Elev: 216ft/66m, Tel: 530-839-2112, Nearest town: Corning. GPS: 39.913849, -122.086749

10 • B3 | Yuba Pass Sno-Park

Dispersed sites, No water, Vault/pit toilet, No tents/RVs: $5, Reservations not accepted, Elev: 6719ft/2048m, Tel: 530-994-3401. GPS: 39.616964, -120.489643

11 • C2 | Austin Creek SRA - Bullfrog Pond

Total sites: 23, RV sites: 23, Central water, No toilets, No showers, No RV dump, Tent & RV camping: $35, Steep, narrow, winding access road - no trailers, Max Length: 20ft, Reservations accepted, Elev: 1286ft/392m, Tel: 707-869-2015, Nearest town: Guerneville. GPS: 38.565927, -123.011085

12 • C2 | Colusa-Sacramento River SRA

Total sites: 12, RV sites: 12, Elec sites: 6, Central water, Flush toilet, Free showers, RV dump, Tents: $28/RVs: $28-38, 3 group sites, Overnight RV parking - 1 night limit $15 - must leave by 0900, Generator hours: 1000-2000, Open all year, Max Length: Trlr-24'/RV-27ft, Reservations accepted, Elev: 66ft/20m, Tel: 530-458-4927, Nearest town: Colusa. GPS: 39.218083, -122.015197

13 • C2 | Lake Oroville SRA - Bidwell Canyon

Total sites: 75, RV sites: 75, Tent & RV camping: $45, Reservations accepted, Elev: 922ft/281m, Tel: 530-538-2218, Nearest town: Oroville. GPS: 39.532781, -121.457922

14 • C2 | Lake Oroville SRA - Forebay Enroute

Dispersed sites, Central water, Flush toilet, Pay showers, RV dump, No tents/RVs: $15, 1-night limit - must leave by 0900, Reservations not accepted, Elev: 237ft/72m, Tel: 530-538-2217, Nearest town: Oroville. GPS: 39.535787, -121.585412

15 • C2 | Lake Oroville SRA - Loafer Creek (Coyote)

Total sites: 137, RV sites: 137, Central water, Flush toilet, Pay showers, RV dump, Tent & RV camping: $25, Open all year, Max Length: RV-40, TRlr-31ft, Reservations accepted, Elev: 994ft/303m, Tel: 530-538-2217, Nearest town: Oroville. GPS: 39.527786, -121.445164

16 • C2 | Lake Oroville SRA - Loafer Creek Horse Camp

Total sites: 12, RV sites: 12, Central water, Vault/pit toilet, Pay showers, RV dump, Tent & RV camping: $45, Open all year, Elev: 978ft/298m, Tel: 530-538-2217, Nearest town: Oroville. GPS: 39.522352, -121.455196

17 • C2 | Sonoma Coast SB - Bodega Dunes

Total sites: 99, RV sites: 99, Central water, Flush toilet, Pay showers, RV dump, Tent & RV camping: $35, Hike/bike: $5, Open all year, Max Length: 31ft, Reservations accepted, Elev: 30ft/9m, Tel: 916-653-6995, Nearest town: Bodega Bay. GPS: 38.337375, -123.055849

18 • C2 | Sonoma Coast SB - Wrights Beach

Total sites: 27, RV sites: 27, No toilets, Tent & RV camping: $35-45, Open all year, Max Length: 31ft, Reservations accepted, Elev: 89ft/27m, Tel: 916-653-6995, Nearest town: Bodega Bay. GPS: 38.400456, -123.095422

19 • C3 | Auburn SRA - Mineral Bar/Iowa Hill Bridge

Total sites: 18, RV sites: 18, No water, Vault/pit toilet, Tent & RV camping: $28, Stay limit: 14 days, Open all year, Reservations not accepted, Elev: 1174ft/358m, Tel: 530-885-4527, Nearest town: Colfax. GPS: 39.101083, -120.923931

20 • C3 | Carson Pass Sno-Park

Dispersed sites, No water, No toilets, No tents/RVs: $5, Sno-Park permit required 1 Nov to 30 May, Stay limit: 14 days, Open all year, Reservations not accepted, Elev: 8671ft/2643m, Tel: 209-295-4251, Nearest town: Kirkwood. GPS: 38.695139, -119.989565

21 • C3 | Donner Summit Sno-Park

Dispersed sites, No water, Vault/pit toilet, No tents/RVs: $5, Sno-Park permit required 1 Nov to 30 May, Open all year, Reservations not accepted, Elev: 7241ft/2207m, Tel: 530-587-3558., Nearest town: Donner. GPS: 39.339639, -120.343386

22 • C3 | Echo Lake Sno-Park

Dispersed sites, No water, Vault/pit toilet, No tents/RVs: $5, Sno-Park permit required 1 Nov to 30 May, Open all year, Reservations not accepted, Elev: 7418ft/2261m, Tel: 530-543-2600., Nearest town: Echo Lake. GPS: 38.823668, -120.033778

23 • C3 | Folsom Lake SRA - Beals Point

Total sites: 69, RV sites: 44, Elec sites: 20, Central water, Flush toilet, Free showers, RV dump, Tents: $28/RVs: $28-48, Open all year, Max Length: 31ft, Reservations accepted, Elev: 459ft/140m, Tel: 916-988-0205, Nearest town: Folsom. GPS: 38.720712, -121.172246

24 • C3 | Folsom Lake SRA - Peninsula

Total sites: 96, RV sites: 96, Central water, Flush toilet, Free showers, RV dump, Tent & RV camping: $33, Open Apr-Sep, Max Length: RV-24,Trlr-18ft, Reservations accepted, Elev: 581ft/177m, Tel: 916-988-0205, Nearest town: Folsom. GPS: 38.758426, -121.112557

25 • C3 | Highway 108 Sno-Park

Dispersed sites, No water, Vault/pit toilet, No tents/RVs: $5, Sno-Park permit required 1 Nov to 30 May, Stay limit: 14 days, Open all year, Reservations not accepted, Elev: 5971ft/1820m, Tel: 209-965-3434, Nearest town: Arnold. GPS: 38.267054, -119.991761

26 • C3 | Hope Valley Sno-Park

Dispersed sites, No water, Vault/pit toilet, No tents/RVs: $5, Sno-Park permit required 1 Nov to 30 May, Stay limit: 14 days, Open all year, Reservations not accepted, Elev: 7142ft/2177m, Tel: 775-882-2766, Nearest town: Kirkwood. GPS: 38.750755, -119.940942

27 • C3 | Iron Mountain Sno-Park - DPR

Dispersed sites, No water, Vault/pit toilet, No tents/RVs: $5, Sno-Park permit required 1 Nov to 30 May, Stay limit: 14 days, Open all year, Reservations not accepted, Elev: 7441ft/2268m, Tel: 209-295-4251, Nearest town: Kirkwood. GPS: 38.628637, -120.208893

28 • C3 | Meiss Meadow Sno-Park

Dispersed sites, No water, Vault/pit toilet, No tents/RVs: $5, Sno-Park permit required 1 Nov to 30 May, Stay limit: 14 days, Open all year, Reservations not accepted, Elev: 7129ft/2173m, Tel: 209-295-4251, Nearest town: Kirkwood. GPS: 38.748203, -119.939442

29 • C3 | Spicer Sno-Park

Dispersed sites, No water, Vault/pit toilet, No tents/RVs: $5, Sno-Park permit required 1 Nov to 30 May, Stay limit: 14 days, Open all year, Reservations not accepted, Elev: 6762ft/2061m, Tel: 209-795-1381, Nearest town: Bear Valley. GPS: 38.428517, -120.077283

30 • C3 | Tahoe SRA

Total sites: 27, RV sites: 16, Central water, Flush toilet, Free showers, No RV dump, Tent & RV camping: $35, Open May-Sep, Max Length: RV-21, Trlr-15ft, Reservations accepted, Elev: 6280ft/1914m, Tel: 530-525-3345, Nearest town: Tahoe City. GPS: 39.175293, -120.135010

31 • C3 | Taylor Creek Sno-Park

Dispersed sites, No water, Vault/pit toilet, No tents/RVs: $5, Sno-Park permit required 1 Nov to 30 May, Open all year, Reservations not accepted, Elev: 6280ft/1914m, Tel: 530-543-2600, Nearest town: Camp Richardson. GPS: 38.932398, -120.057380

32 • D2 | Benicia SRA

Total sites: 3, RV sites: 3, No water, No toilets, No tents/RVs: $10-15, Must be fully self-contained, Stay limit: 1 day, Open all year, Reservations not accepted, Elev: 16ft/5m, Tel: 707-648-1911, Nearest town: Benicia. GPS: 38.078661, -122.194252

33 • D2 | Brannan Island SRA - Cottonwood

Total sites: 51, RV sites: 51, Central water, Flush toilet, Free showers, RV dump, Tent & RV camping: $31-36, Open all year, Max Length: 36ft, Reservations accepted, Elev: 18ft/5m, Tel: 916-777-6671, Nearest town: Rio Vista. GPS: 38.109517, -121.695087

34 • D2 | Brannan Island SRA - Olympic

Total sites: 12, RV sites: 12, Elec sites: 12, Water at site, Flush toilet, Free showers, RV dump, Tent & RV camping: $49, Open all year, Max Length: 36ft, Reservations accepted, Elev: 23ft/7m, Tel: 916-777-6671, Nearest town: Rio Vista. GPS: 38.115729, -121.690208

35 • D2 | Brannan Island SRA - Willow

Total sites: 50, RV sites: 50, Central water, Flush toilet, Free showers, RV dump, Tent & RV camping: $31-36, Open all year, Max Length: 36ft, Reservations accepted, Elev: 21ft/6m, Tel: 916-777-6671, Nearest town: Rio Vista. GPS: 38.112796, -121.692874

36 • D2 | Carnegie SVRA

Total sites: 23, RV sites: 23, Central water, Flush toilet, Pay showers, No RV dump, Tent & RV camping: $10, Reservations not accepted, Elev: 636ft/194m, Tel: 925-447-9027, Nearest town: Tracy. GPS: 37.628174, -121.528564

37 • D2 | Half Moon Bay SB - Francis Beach

Total sites: 52, RV sites: 47, Elec sites: 36, Central water, Flush toilet, Free showers, RV dump, Tents: $35/RVs: $35-65, Group site: $165, Bike-in $7, Open all year, Max Length: 40ft, Elev: 26ft/8m, Tel: 650-726-8819, Nearest town: Half Moon Bay. GPS: 37.468566, -122.445809

38 • D3 | George J Hatfield SRA

Total sites: 21, RV sites: 21, Central water, No toilets, No showers, No RV dump, Tent & RV camping: $20, Group site:

$150, Generator hours: 0800-2200, Reservations not accepted, Elev: 102ft/31m, Tel: 209-632-2852, Nearest town: Hilmar. GPS: 37.351766, -120.959663

39 • D3 | McConnell SRA

Total sites: 19, RV sites: 19, Flush toilet, Free showers, Tent & RV camping: $30, 2 group sites $100-$150, Reservations accepted, Elev: 121ft/37m, Tel: 209-394-7755, Nearest town: Ballico. GPS: 37.416027, -120.710835

40 • D3 | Turlock Lake SRA

Total sites: 66, RV sites: 30, Central water, Flush toilet, Free showers, No RV dump, Tent & RV camping: $36, Open all year, Max Length: RV-27ft, Trlr-24ft, Reservations accepted, Elev: 148ft/45m, Tel: 209-874-2056, Nearest town: La Grange. GPS: 37.630434, -120.581672

41 • D4 | Balsam Meadows Sno-Park

Dispersed sites, No water, Vault/pit toilet, No tents/RVs: $5, Sno-Park permit required 1 Nov to 30 May, Open all year, Reservations not accepted, Elev: 6722ft/2049m, Tel: 559-841-3194, Nearest town: Big Creek. GPS: 37.159386, -119.242733

42 • D4 | Coyote Sno-Park

Dispersed sites, No water, Vault/pit toilet, No tents/RVs: $5, Sno-Park permit required 1 Nov to 30 May, Open all year, Elev: 7510ft/2289m, Tel: 559-855-5355, Nearest town: Big Creek. GPS: 37.167030, -119.205933

43 • D4 | Eastwood Sno-Park

Dispersed sites, No water, Vault/pit toilet, No tents/RVs: $5, Sno-Park permit required 1 Nov to 30 May, Open all year, Reservations not accepted, Elev: 7037ft/2145m, Tel: 559-855-5355, Nearest town: Lakeshore. GPS: 37.255807, -119.160867

44 • D4 | Huntington Lake Sno-Park

Dispersed sites, No water, No toilets, No tents/RVs: $5, Sno-Park permit required 1 Nov to 30 May, Open all year, Reservations not accepted, Elev: 7037ft/2145m, Tel: 559-855-5355, Nearest town: Lakeshore. GPS: 37.251416, -119.174213

45 • D4 | Rock Creek Sno-Park

Dispersed sites, No water, Vault/pit toilet, No tents/RVs: $5, Sno-Park permit required 1 Nov to 30 May, Stay limit: 28 days, Open all year, Reservations not accepted, Elev: 8921ft/2719m, Tel: 760-873-2500, Nearest town: Mesa. GPS: 37.494392, -118.717439

46 • D4 | Tamarack Sno-Park

Dispersed sites, No water, Vault/pit toilet, No tents/RVs: $5, Sno-Park permit required 1 Nov to 30 May, Open all year, Reservations not accepted, Elev: 7651ft/2332m, Tel: 559-855-5355, Nearest town: Big Creek. GPS: 37.162431, -119.201864

47 • E1 | Hollister Hills SVRA

Total sites: 125, RV sites: 125, No water, Flush toilet, Tent & RV camping: $10, Group fee: $250, Max Length: RV-26, Trlr-18ft, Reservations not accepted, Elev: 843ft/257m, Tel: 831-637-3874, Nearest town: Hollister. GPS: 36.768311, -121.411865

48 • E1 | New Brighton SB

Total sites: 111, RV sites: 111, Elec sites: 10, Central water, Flush toilet, Free showers, RV dump, Tents: $35/RVs: $35-50, Group site $185, Reservations accepted, Elev: 151ft/46m, Tel: 831-464-6330, Nearest town: Capitola. GPS: 36.980997, -121.933441

49 • E1 | San Luis Reservoir SRA - Basalt

Total sites: 79, RV sites: 79, Central water, Flush toilet, Free showers, No RV dump, Tent & RV camping: $30, Open all year, Reservations accepted, Elev: 623ft/190m, Tel: 209-826-1197. GPS: 37.027662, -121.064203

50 • E1 | San Luis Reservoir SRA - Los Banos Creek

Total sites: 15, RV sites: 13, Central water, Flush toilet, Free showers, RV dump, Tent & RV camping: $20-25, Open all year, Reservations accepted, Elev: 364ft/111m, Tel: 209-826-1197, Nearest town: Gustine. GPS: 36.986565, -120.939095

51 • E1 | San Luis Reservoir SRA - Medeiros

Total sites: 16, RV sites: 16, No toilets, Tent & RV camping: $20-25, Open all year, Reservations accepted, Elev: 246ft/75m, Tel: 209-826-1197. GPS: 37.065577, -121.030684

52 • E1 | San Luis Reservoir SRA - San Luis Creek

Total sites: 49, RV sites: 49, Elec sites: 49, Central water, Flush toilet, Free showers, RV dump, Tent & RV camping: $40, 2 group sites $100-$200, Open all year, Reservations accepted, Elev: 2325ft/709m, Tel: 209-826-1197, Nearest town: Gustine. GPS: 37.108422, -121.065336

53 • E1 | Seacliff SB

Total sites: 35, RV sites: 35, Central water, Flush toilet, Free showers, No RV dump, No tents/RVs: $55-65, No fires, Open all year, Reservations accepted, Elev: 112ft/34m, Tel: 831-685-6442, Nearest town: Aptos. GPS: 36.973159, -121.916217

54 • E1 | Sunset SB

Total sites: 90, RV sites: 90, Central water, Flush toilet, Pay showers, No RV dump, Tent & RV camping: $35, Group site $335, Open all year, Max Length: 31ft, Reservations accepted, Elev: 141ft/43m, Tel: 831-763-7062, Nearest town: Watsonville. GPS: 36.889028, -121.830041

55 • E2 | Millerton Lake SRA - Horse Camp

Total sites: Unk, RV sites: Unk, Central water, Flush toilet, Free showers, RV dump, Tent & RV camping: Fee unk, Open all year, Elev: 583ft/178m, Tel: 559-822-2332, Nearest town: Friant. GPS: 37.022434, -119.668036

56 • E2 | Millerton Lake SRA - Meadows

Total sites: 58, RV sites: 58, Elec sites: 25, Central water, Flush toilet, Free showers, RV dump, Tents: $30/RVs: $30-40, 22 Full hookups, Open all year, Max Length: 36ft, Reservations accepted, Elev: 581ft/177m, Tel: 559-822-2332, Nearest town: Friant. GPS: 37.019985, -119.668016

57 • E2 | Millerton Lake SRA - Rocky Pt, Mono, Ft Miller, Duma Strand

Total sites: 84, RV sites: 51, Central water, Flush toilet, Free showers, RV dump, Tent & RV camping: $30, 2 Group sites $150-

$200, Open all year, Max Length: 36ft, Reservations accepted, Elev: 607ft/185m, Tel: 559-822-2332, Nearest town: Friant. GPS: 37.022278, -119.683357

58 • E2 | Millerton Lake SRA - Valley Oak

Total sites: 6, RV sites: 6, Central water, Flush toilet, Free showers, RV dump, Tent & RV camping: $30, Open all year, Elev: 599ft/183m, Tel: 559-822-2332, Nearest town: Friant. GPS: 37.021975, -119.665994

59 • F1 | Morro Strand SB

Total sites: 76, RV sites: 76, Elec sites: 25, Water at site, Flush toilet, No showers, No RV dump, Tents: $35/RVs: $35-50, 25 Full hookups, Showers available at Morro Bay SP, Generator hours: 1000-2200, Max Length: 40ft, Reservations accepted, Elev: 46ft/14m, Tel: 805-772-2560, Nearest town: Morro Bay. GPS: 35.400427, -120.866815

60 • F2 | Oceano Dunes SVRA

Total sites: 80, RV sites: 80, Central water, Flush toilet, Free showers, RV dump, Tent & RV camping: $10, 4x4 recommended, Beach camping, Open all year, Max Length: 40ft, Elev: 30ft/9m, Tel: 805-473-7220, Nearest town: Oceano. GPS: 35.092697, -120.616668

61 • F2 | Pismo SB - North Beach

Total sites: 102, RV sites: 102, Central water, Flush toilet, Free showers, RV dump, Tent & RV camping: $35, Generator hours: 0800-2000, Open all year, Max Length: RV-36, Trlr-31ft, Reservations accepted, Elev: 23ft/7m, Nearest town: Oceano. GPS: 35.130728, -120.634956

62 • F2 | Pismo SB - Oceano

Total sites: 82, RV sites: 82, Elec sites: 42, Central water, Flush toilet, Free showers, Tent & RV camping: $35-50, Generator hours: 0800-2000, Reservations accepted, Elev: 16ft/5m, Tel: 805-473-7220, Nearest town: Oceano. GPS: 35.107799, -120.627477

63 • F5 | Providence Mountains SRA

Total sites: 6, RV sites: 2, Central water, Flush toilet, No showers, Tent & RV camping: $25, Walk-to sites, Max Length: 30ft, Elev: 4270ft/1301m, Tel: 760-928-2586, Nearest town: Essex. GPS: 34.943394, -115.512149

64 • G2 | El Capitan SB

Total sites: 132, RV sites: 132, Central water, Flush toilet, Pay showers, No RV dump, Tent & RV camping: $45, Group sites: $225-$320, Open all year, Max Length: 42ft, Reservations accepted, Elev: 30ft/9m, Tel: 805-968-1033, Nearest town: Goleta. GPS: 34.461914, -120.021973

65 • G2 | Emma Wood SB

Total sites: 90, RV sites: 90, No water, No toilets, No tents/RVs: $40, Self-contained vehicles only, Sites not level, Group sites: $130-$360, Near RR, One-night-only enroute camping at Ventura River Group Camp 2 miles south, Open all year, Max Length: 45ft, Reservations accepted, Elev: 148ft/45m, Tel: 805-968-1033, Nearest town: Ventura. GPS: 34.291313, -119.337643

66 • G2 | McGrath SB

Total sites: 173, RV sites: 173, Central water, Flush toilet, Free showers, RV dump, Tent & RV camping: $45, Hike/bike: $10, Reservations accepted, Elev: 20ft/6m, Tel: 805-654-4744, Nearest town: Oxnard. GPS: 34.227126, -119.258061

67 • G2 | Refugio SB

Total sites: 67, RV sites: 67, Central water, Flush toilet, Free showers, No RV dump, Tent & RV camping: $45, Hike/bike: $10, 3 group sites $235-$350, Open all year, Max Length: RV-30, Trlr-27ft, Reservations accepted, Elev: 10ft/3m, Tel: 805-968-1033, Nearest town: Goleta. GPS: 34.464066, -120.069754

68 • G3 | Bolsa Chica SB

Total sites: 57, RV sites: 57, Water at site, Flush toilet, Free showers, RV dump, No tents/RVs: $55-65, Open all year, Max Length: 40ft, Reservations accepted, Elev: -13ft/-4m, Tel: 714-846-3460, Nearest town: Huntington Beach. GPS: 33.691319, -118.043662

69 • G3 | Castaic Lake SRA

Total sites: 25, RV sites: 25, Vault/pit toilet, RV dump, Tent & RV camping: $20, Open Thu-Sun, Open May-Sep, Reservations not accepted, Elev: 1250ft/381m, Tel: 661-257-4050, Nearest town: Castaic. GPS: 34.505782, -118.606921

70 • G3 | Hungry Valley SVRA - Alkilik

Total sites: 15, RV sites: 15, No water, Vault/pit toilet, Tent & RV camping: $10, Reservations not accepted, Elev: 3389ft/1033m, Tel: 661-248-7007, Nearest town: Gorman. GPS: 34.722703, -118.863758

71 • G3 | Hungry Valley SVRA - Circle Canyon

Total sites: 21, RV sites: 21, No water, Vault/pit toilet, Tent & RV camping: $10, Reservations not accepted, Elev: 4022ft/1226m, Tel: 661-248-7007, Nearest town: Gorman. GPS: 34.761792, -118.868865

72 • G3 | Hungry Valley SVRA - Cottonwood

Total sites: 14, RV sites: 14, No water, Vault/pit toilet, Tent & RV camping: $10, Reservations not accepted, Elev: 3963ft/1208m, Tel: 661-248-7007, Nearest town: Gorman. GPS: 34.759529, -118.881362

73 • G3 | Hungry Valley SVRA - Edison Canyon

Total sites: 13, RV sites: 13, No water, Vault/pit toilet, Tent & RV camping: $10, Reservations not accepted, Elev: 4134ft/1260m, Tel: 661-248-7007, Nearest town: Gorman. GPS: 34.772355, -118.878743

74 • G3 | Hungry Valley SVRA - Lane Ranch

Total sites: 20, RV sites: 20, No water, Vault/pit toilet, Tent & RV camping: $10, 1 group site, Reservations not accepted, Elev: 3215ft/980m, Tel: 661-248-7007, Nearest town: Gorman. GPS: 34.721806, -118.846072

75 • G3 | Hungry Valley SVRA - Lower Scrub Oaks

Total sites: 10, RV sites: 10, No water, Vault/pit toilet, Tent & RV camping: $10, Reservations not accepted, Elev: 3655ft/1114m, Tel: 661-248-7007, Nearest town: Gorman. GPS: 34.745047, -118.874055

76 • G3 | Hungry Valley SVRA - Smith Forks

Total sites: 35, RV sites: 35, No water, Vault/pit toilet, Tent & RV camping: $10, 2 group sites, Reservations not accepted, Elev: 3481ft/1061m, Tel: 661-248-7007, Nearest town: Gorman. GPS: 34.730048, -118.868749

77 • G3 | Hungry Valley SVRA - Sterling Canyon

Total sites: 15, RV sites: 15, No water, Vault/pit toilet, Tent & RV camping: $10, Reservations not accepted, Elev: 4017ft/1224m, Tel: 661-248-7007, Nearest town: Gorman. GPS: 34.766132, -118.878792

78 • G3 | Hungry Valley SVRA - Upper Scrub Oaks

Total sites: 18, RV sites: 18, No water, Vault/pit toilet, Tent & RV camping: $10, Reservations not accepted, Elev: 3766ft/1148m, Tel: 661-248-7007, Nearest town: Gorman. GPS: 34.750836, -118.877704

79 • G4 | Lake Perris SRA - Coyote

Total sites: 102, RV sites: 102, Elec sites: 102, Water at site, Flush toilet, Free showers, RV dump, No tents/RVs: $45, Open all year, Reservations accepted, Elev: 1642ft/500m, Tel: 951-940-5600, Nearest town: Perris. GPS: 33.872375, -117.176329

80 • G4 | Lake Perris SRA - Deer

Total sites: 161, RV sites: 161, Elec sites: 161, Water at site, Flush toilet, Free showers, RV dump, No tents/RVs: $45, Open May-Oct, Reservations accepted, Elev: 1649ft/503m, Tel: 951-940-5600, Nearest town: Perris. GPS: 33.874931, -117.173928

81 • G4 | Lake Perris SRA - Horse Camp

Total sites: 7, RV sites: 7, Central water, Vault/pit toilet, No showers, No RV dump, Tent & RV camping: $25, Open all year, Max Length: 31ft, Reservations accepted, Elev: 1785ft/544m, Tel: 951-940-5600, Nearest town: Perris. GPS: 33.877771, -117.180648

82 • G4 | Silverwood Lake SRA - Mesa

Total sites: 134, RV sites: 134, Elec sites: 39, Water available, Flush toilet, Pay showers, RV dump, Tent & RV camping: $45, 7 group sites $150-$325, Open all year, Max Length: RV-32ft, Trlr-31ft, Reservations accepted, Elev: 3497ft/1066m, Tel: 760-389-2281, Nearest town: Hesperia. GPS: 34.284281, -117.351522

83 • H3 | Doheny SB

Total sites: 122, RV sites: 122, Central water, Flush toilet, Free showers, RV dump, Tents: $40/RVs: $40-60, Goup site: $300, Max Length: 35ft, Reservations accepted, Elev: 33ft/10m, Tel: 949-496-6172, Nearest town: Dana Point. GPS: 33.462336, -117.680587

84 • H3 | San Clemente SB

Total sites: 160, RV sites: 72, Elec sites: 72, Water at site, Flush toilet, Free showers, RV dump, Tents: $40/RVs: $40-65, 72 Full hookups, 2 group sites $250-$300, Open all year, Max Length: 30ft, Reservations accepted, Elev: 161ft/49m, Tel: 949-492-3156, Nearest town: San Clemente. GPS: 33.404662, -117.600801

85 • H3 | San Onofre SB - Bluffs CG

Total sites: 16, RV sites: 9, Central water, Flush toilet, Free showers, RV dump, Tent & RV camping: $40, Cold showers, 1 group site $250, Open May-Sep, Max Length: 36ft, Elev: 46ft/14m, Tel:

949-492-4872, Nearest town: San Clemente. GPS: 33.377476, -117.570251

86 • H3 | San Onofre SB - San Meteo CG

Total sites: 157, RV sites: 157, Central water, Flush toilet, Pay showers, RV dump, Tents: $40/RVs: $40-65, 1 group site $200, Open all year, Max Length: 36ft, Elev: 102ft/31m, Tel: 949-492-4872, Nearest town: San Clemente. GPS: 33.406570, -117.584830

87 • H4 | Ocotillo Wells SVRA

Dispersed sites, No water, Flush toilet, Pay showers, Tent & RV camping: Free, Open all year, Reservations not accepted, Elev: 256ft/78m, Tel: 760-767-5391, Nearest town: Ocotillo Wells. GPS: 33.157227, -116.149658

88 • H4 | Salton Sea SRA - New Camp

Total sites: 26, RV sites: 26, Elec sites: 4, Central water, Flush toilet, Pay showers, RV dump, Tents: $20/RVs: $20-30, Solar showers, Open all year, Reservations accepted, Elev: -210ft/-64m, Tel: 760-393-3052, Nearest town: Mecca. GPS: 33.501481, -115.911836

89 • H4 | Salton Sea SRA -Corvina Beach

Dispersed sites, Central water, Vault/pit toilet, Free showers, Tent & RV camping: $10, Cold showers, Firewood collection not allowed, Open Oct-May, Max Length: 60+ft, Reservations not accepted, Elev: -200ft/-61m, Tel: 760-393-3052, Nearest town: Mecca. GPS: 33.477725, -115.890954

90 • H4 | Salton Sea SRA -Headquarters

Total sites: 15, RV sites: 15, Elec sites: 15, Central water, Flush toilet, Pay showers, RV dump, No tents/RVs: $30, 15 Full hookups, Open all year, Max Length: 40ft, Reservations accepted, Elev: -194ft/-59m, Tel: 760-393-3052, Nearest town: Mecca. GPS: 33.504137, -115.913670

91 • H4 | Salton Sea SRA -Mecca Beach

Total sites: 109, RV sites: 109, Elec sites: 4, Central water, Flush toilet, Free showers, Tents: $20/RVs: $20-30, Solar showers, Open Oct-May, Max Length: 45ft, Reservations not accepted, Elev: -207ft/-63m, Tel: 760-393-3052, Nearest town: Mecca. GPS: 33.490249, -115.901803

92 • H4 | Salton Sea SRA -Salt Creek Beach

Total sites: 200, RV sites: 200, Central water, Vault/pit toilet, No showers, No RV dump, Tent & RV camping: $10, Open Oct-May, Elev: -216ft/-66m, Tel: 760-393-3052, Nearest town: Mecca. GPS: 33.444261, -115.846523

93 • H4 | San Elijo SB

Total sites: 171, RV sites: 171, Elec sites: 26, Central water, Flush toilet, Free showers, RV dump, Tent & RV camping: $35-75, Dump fee: $10-$20, Open all year, Max Length: 35ft, Reservations accepted, Elev: 59ft/18m, Tel: 760-753-5091, Nearest town: Cardiff. GPS: 33.021014, -117.284343

94 • H4 | Silver Strand SB

Total sites: 140, RV sites: 140, Central water, No toilets, RV dump, No tents/RVs: $50-65, RVs must be self-contained, Dump fee: $10-$20, Stay limit: 7 days, Open all year, Reservations accepted,

Elev: 10ft/3m, Tel: 619-435-5184, Nearest town: Coronado. GPS: 32.636208, -117.143009

95 • H4 | South Carlsbad SB

Total sites: 223, RV sites: 223, Elec sites: 14, Central water, Flush toilet, Pay showers, RV dump, Tents: $35-75/RVs: $35-100, Dump fee: $10-$20, Generator hours: 1000-2000, Open all year, Max Length: 35-75ft, Reservations accepted, Elev: 62ft/19m, Tel: 760-438-3143, Nearest town: Carlsbad. GPS: 33.104004, -117.319336

96 • H5 | Picacho SRA - 4S Beach CG

Dispersed sites, Central water, Flush toilet, Free showers, No RV dump, Tent & RV camping: $25, 4x4 recommended, solar showers, Reservations not accepted, Elev: 180ft/55m, Tel: 760-996-2963, Nearest town: Winterhaven. GPS: 33.055768, -114.676233

97 • H5 | Picacho SRA - Main CG

Total sites: 54, RV sites: 54, Central water, Vault/pit toilet, Free showers, RV dump, Tent & RV camping: $20, Solar showers, 1 group site $75, Reservations not accepted, Elev: 203ft/62m, Tel: 760-996-2963, Nearest town: Winterhaven. GPS: 33.022545, -114.617992

98 • H5 | Picacho SRA - Taylor Lake CG

Dispersed sites, Central water, Flush toilet, Free showers, No RV dump, Tent & RV camping: $20, Solar showers, Reservations not accepted, Elev: 194ft/59m, Tel: 760-996-2963, Nearest town: Winterhaven. GPS: 33.029355, -114.637791

99 • H5 | Picacho SRA - The Outpost CG

Dispersed sites, Central water, Flush toilet, Free showers, No RV dump, Tent & RV camping: $25, 4x4 recommended, solar showers, Reservations not accepted, Elev: 203ft/62m, Tel: 760-996-2963, Nearest town: Winterhaven. GPS: 33.069020, -114.687323

Colorado

NEBRASKA

KANSAS

WYOMING

UTAH

OKLAHOMA

NEW MEXICO

AZ

COLORADO

Sterling

Burlington

Lamar

Limon

Fort Collins

Colorado Springs

Pueblo

Trinidad

Denver

Alamosa

Craig

Grand Junction

Montrose

Durango

1,2,5

8,9,20,21

17,18

11,13,14,24

16

7

6,19

3,10,12,15

4,22,23

34, 70, 287, 76, 50, 34, 25, 25, 24, 160, 50, 285, 285, 160, 40, 13, 13, 70, 550, 50, 40, 160

Map	ID	Map	ID
C3	1-24		

Alphabetical List of Camping Areas

1 • C3 | Arkansas Headwaters SRA - 5 1/2 Points Dispersed

Dispersed sites, No water, No toilets, Tent & RV camping: Free, Must provide own fire ring and human waste removal means, Open all year, Elev: 5946ft/1812m, Tel: 719-539-7289, Nearest town: Canon City. GPS: 38.456783, -105.486599

2 • C3 | Arkansas Headwaters SRA - Bootlegger Dispersed

Dispersed sites, No water, No toilets, Tent & RV camping: Free, Walk-to sites, No large RVs, Must provide own fire ring and human waste removal means, Open all year, Elev: 5880ft/1792m, Tel: 719-539-7289, Nearest town: Canon City. GPS: 38.466167, -105.452216

3 • C3 | Arkansas Headwaters SRA - Boulderfield Dispersed

Dispersed sites, No water, No toilets, Tent & RV camping: Free, Also boat-in sites, Nothing larger than van/PU, Must provide own fire ring and human waste removal means, Open all year, Elev: 8377ft/2553m, Tel: 719-539-7289, Nearest town: Buena Vista. GPS: 38.943245, -106.185839

4 • C3 | Arkansas Headwaters SRA - Elephant Rock Dispersed

Dispersed sites, No water, No toilets, Tent & RV camping: Free, Must provide own fire ring and human waste removal means, Open all year, Elev: 8117ft/2474m, Tel: 719-539-7289, Nearest town: Buena Vista. GPS: 38.884661, -106.152148

5 • C3 | Arkansas Headwaters SRA - Five Points

Total sites: 20, RV sites: 20, No water, Vault/pit toilet, Tent & RV camping: $28, $9 daily entrance fee, Open all year, Max Length: 50ft, Reservations required, Elev: 5965ft/1818m, Tel: 719-539-7289, Nearest town: Parkdale. GPS: 38.452989, -105.493149

6 • C3 | Arkansas Headwaters SRA - Granite Rock Dispersed

Dispersed sites, No water, No toilets, Tent & RV camping: Free, Must provide own fire ring and human waste removal means, Open all year, Elev: 8996ft/2742m, Tel: 719-539-7289, Nearest town: Granite. GPS: 39.033299, -106.252797

7 • C3 | Arkansas Headwaters SRA - Hecla Junction

Total sites: 22, RV sites: 19, No water, Vault/pit toilet, Tent & RV camping: $28, $9 daily entrance fee, Open all year, Reservations required, Elev: 7444ft/2269m, Tel: 719-539-7289, Nearest town: Salida. GPS: 38.652951, -106.051508

8 • C3 | Arkansas Headwaters SRA - Lazy J Dispersed

Dispersed sites, No water, No toilets, Tent & RV camping: Free, Must provide own fire ring and human waste removal means, Open all year, Elev: 6175ft/1882m, Tel: 719-539-7289, Nearest town: Canon City. GPS: 38.417359, -105.574734

9 • C3 | Arkansas Headwaters SRA - Maytag Dispersed

Dispersed sites, No water, No toilets, Tent & RV camping: Free, Must provide own fire ring and human waste removal means, Reservations not accepted, Elev: 6159ft/1877m, Tel: 719-269-8500, Nearest town: Canon City. GPS: 38.425779, -105.567022

10 • C3 | Arkansas Headwaters SRA - Railroad Bridge

Total sites: 14, RV sites: 7, No water, Vault/pit toilet, Tent & RV camping: $28, $9 daily entrance fee, Open all year, Reservations required, Elev: 8269ft/2520m, Tel: 719-539-7289, Nearest town: Buena Vista. GPS: 38.922878, -106.170016

11 • C3 | Arkansas Headwaters SRA - Rainbow Route Dispersed

Dispersed sites, No water, No toilets, Tent & RV camping: Free, Must provide own fire ring and human waste removal means, Open all year, Elev: 6795ft/2071m, Tel: 719-539-7289, Nearest town: Wellsville. GPS: 38.473575, -105.878223

12 • C3 | Arkansas Headwaters SRA - Rapid #6 Dispersed

Dispersed sites, No water, No toilets, Tent & RV camping: Free, Also boat-in sites, Nothing larger than van/PU, Must provide own fire ring and human waste removal means, Open all year, Elev: 8370ft/2551m, Tel: 719-539-7289, Nearest town: Buena Vista. GPS: 38.942518, -106.184549

13 • C3 | Arkansas Headwaters SRA - Red Wall Dispersed

Dispersed sites, No water, No toilets, Tent & RV camping: Free, Must provide own fire ring and human waste removal means, Open all year, Elev: 6801ft/2073m, Tel: 719-539-7289, Nearest town: Wellsville. GPS: 38.475597, -105.881126

14 • C3 | Arkansas Headwaters SRA - Rincon

Total sites: 8, RV sites: 8, No water, Vault/pit toilet, Tent & RV camping: $28, $9 daily entrance fee, Open all year, Max Length: 50ft, Reservations required, Elev: 6857ft/2090m, Tel: 719-539-7289, Nearest town: Wellsville. GPS: 38.470814, -105.865114

15 • C3 | Arkansas Headwaters SRA - Riverside Dispersed

Dispersed sites, No water, No toilets, Tent & RV camping: Free, Must provide own fire ring and human waste removal means, Open all year, Elev: 8299ft/2530m, Tel: 719-539-7289, Nearest town: Buena Vista. GPS: 38.930941, -106.172439

16 • C3 | Arkansas Headwaters SRA - Ruby Mountain

Total sites: 22, RV sites: 12, No water, Vault/pit toilet, Tent & RV camping: $28, $9 daily entrance fee, Open all year, Max Length: 40ft, Reservations required, Elev: 7694ft/2345m, Tel: 719-539-7289, Nearest town: Buena Vista. GPS: 38.752879, -106.069714

17 • C3 | Arkansas Headwaters SRA - Salida East

Total sites: 16, RV sites: 16, No water, Vault/pit toilet, Tent & RV camping: $28, $9 daily entrance fee, Open all year, Max Length: 50ft, Reservations required, Elev: 6997ft/2133m, Tel: 719-539-7289, Nearest town: Salida. GPS: 38.507711, -105.960703

18 • C3 | Arkansas Headwaters SRA - Salidas East North Dispersed

Dispersed sites, No water, No toilets, Tent & RV camping: Free, Must provide own fire ring and human waste removal means, Open all year, Elev: 6988ft/2130m, Tel: 719-539-7289, Nearest town: Salida. GPS: 38.510523, -105.964467

19 • C3 | Arkansas Headwaters SRA - Stone Cabin Dispersed

Dispersed sites, No water, No toilets, Tent & RV camping: Free, Must provide own fire ring and human waste removal means, Open all year, Elev: 8873ft/2704m, Tel: 719-539-7289, Nearest town: Granite. GPS: 39.020002, -106.240225

20 • C3 | Arkansas Headwaters SRA - Texas Creek OHV Dispersed

Dispersed sites, No water, No toilets, Tent & RV camping: Free, Must provide own fire ring and human waste removal means, Open Sep-May, Elev: 6291ft/1917m, Tel: 719-269-8500, Nearest town: Canon City. GPS: 38.415728, -105.586324

21 • C3 | Arkansas Headwaters SRA - Texas Creek West Dispersed

Dispersed sites, No water, No toilets, Tent & RV camping: Free, Must provide own fire ring and human waste removal means, Open all year, Elev: 6254ft/1906m, Tel: 719-539-7289, Nearest town: Canon City. GPS: 38.413139, -105.601784

22 • C3 | Arkansas Headwaters SRA - Tunnel View Dispersed

Dispersed sites, No water, No toilets, Tent & RV camping: Free, Several sites along road, Must provide own fire ring and human waste removal means, Elev: 8070ft/2460m, Nearest town: Buena Vista. GPS: 38.872347, -106.147037

23 • C3 | Arkansas Headwaters SRA - Tunnel View Dispersed

Dispersed sites, No water, No toilets, Tent & RV camping: Free, Must provide own fire ring and human waste removal means, Open all year, Elev: 8089ft/2466m, Tel: 719-539-7289, Nearest town: Buena Vista. GPS: 38.868667, -106.147427

24 • C3 | Arkansas Headwaters SRA - Woody's Claim Dispersed

Dispersed sites, No water, No toilets, Tent & RV camping: Free, Must provide own fire ring and human waste removal means, Open all year, Elev: 6812ft/2076m, Tel: 719-539-7289, Nearest town: Salida. GPS: 38.476576, -105.885998

Florida

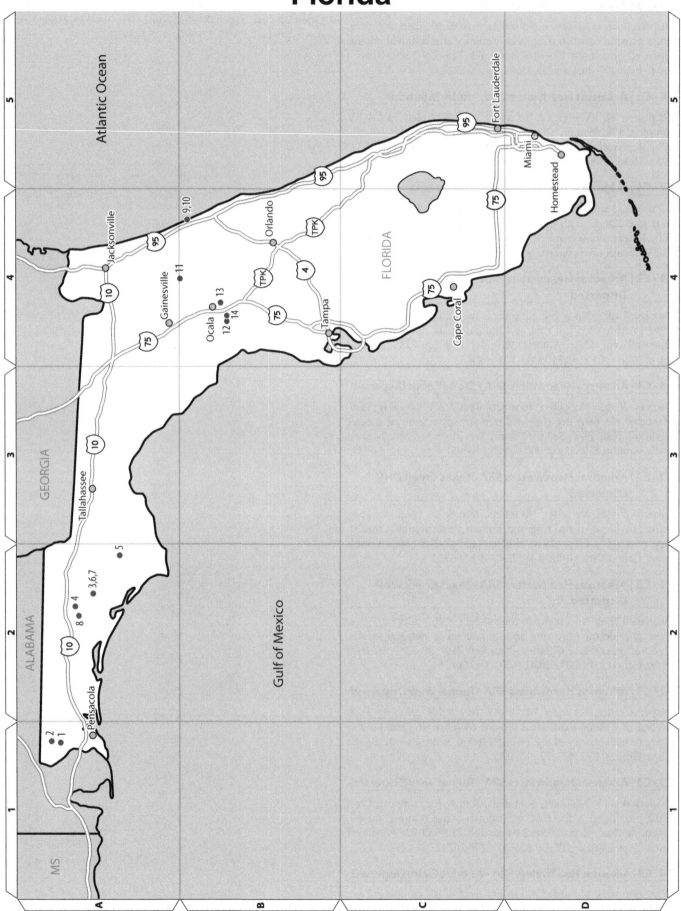

Map	ID	Map	ID
A1	1-2	B4	9-14
A2	3-8		

Alphabetical List of Camping Areas

1 • A1 | Cotton Lake - NWFWMD

Total sites: 7, RV sites: 4, No water, Vault/pit toilet, Tent & RV camping: Donation, Reservations required, Elev: 20ft/6m, Tel: 850-539-5999, Nearest town: Molino. GPS: 30.784753, -87.314212

2 • A1 | Williams Lake - NWFWMD

Dispersed sites, No water, Vault/pit toilet, Tent & RV camping: Donation, Reservations required, Elev: 33ft/10m, Tel: 850-539-5999, Nearest town: Jay. GPS: 30.877739, -87.292173

3 • A2 | Blue Spring - NWFWMD

Dispersed sites, No water, Vault/pit toilet, Tent & RV camping: Free, Reservations required, Elev: 42ft/13m, Tel: 850-539-5999, Nearest town: Youngstown. GPS: 30.453266, -85.529713

4 • A2 | Cotton Landing Rec Area - NWFWMD

Total sites: 3, RV sites: 3, Vault/pit toilet, Tent & RV camping: Donation, Max Length: 18ft, Reservations required, Elev: 32ft/10m, Nearest town: Vernon. GPS: 30.655857, -85.680892

5 • A2 | Florida River Island - NWFWMD

Total sites: 10, RV sites: 4, No water, Vault/pit toilet, Tent & RV camping: Donation, Reservations accepted, Elev: 36ft/11m, Tel: 850-539-5999, Nearest town: Bristol. GPS: 30.184437, -85.085004

6 • A2 | Rattlesnake Lake North - NWFWMD

Dispersed sites, No water, Vault/pit toilet, Tent & RV camping: Donation, Open Feb-Nov, Reservations required, Elev: 51ft/16m, Tel: 850-539-5999, Nearest town: Fountain. GPS: 30.461166, -85.563945

7 • A2 | Sparkleberry Pond - NWFWMD

Dispersed sites, No water, Vault/pit toilet, Tent & RV camping: Free, Reservations required, Elev: 49ft/15m, Nearest town: Youngstown. GPS: 30.461145, -85.520822

8 • A2 | Spurling Landing Recreation Area - NWFWMD

Dispersed sites, Vault/pit toilet, Tent & RV camping: Donation, Tents-vans-pickup campers only, Reservations required, Elev: 30ft/9m, Nearest town: Vernon. GPS: 30.606486, -85.807654

9 • B4 | Gamble Rogers SRA - Beach

Total sites: 34, RV sites: 34, Elec sites: 34, Water at site, Flush toilet, Free showers, RV dump, Tent & RV camping: $28, Stay limit: 14 days, Open all year, Reservations accepted, Elev: 13ft/4m, Tel: 386-517-2086, Nearest town: Flagler Beach. GPS: 29.437682, -81.107585

10 • B4 | Gamble Rogers SRA - Riverside

Total sites: 34, RV sites: 30, Elec sites: 34, Water at site, Flush toilet, Free showers, RV dump, Tent & RV camping: $28, Stay limit: 14 days, Open all year, Reservations accepted, Elev: 8ft/2m, Tel: 386-517-2086, Nearest town: Flagler Beach. GPS: 29.439832, -81.112122

11 • B4 | Marjorie Harris Carr Cross-Florida Greenway - Rodman

Total sites: 67, RV sites: 27, Elec sites: 27, Central water, RV dump, Tents: $12/RVs: $29, Open all year, Elev: 56ft/17m, Tel: 386-326-2846, Nearest town: Palatka. GPS: 29.527254, -81.791615

12 • B4 | Marjorie Harris Carr Cross-Florida Greenway - Ross Prairie

Total sites: 14, RV sites: 14, Elec sites: 14, Water at site, Flush toilet, Free showers, Tents: $22/RVs: $29, Open all year, Reservations accepted, Elev: 59ft/18m, Tel: 352-732-2606, Nearest town: Dunnellon. GPS: 29.039461, -82.296192

13 • B4 | Marjorie Harris Carr Cross-Florida Greenway - Santos

Total sites: 24, RV sites: 24, Elec sites: 24, Water at site, Flush toilet, Free showers, RV dump, Tents: $22/RVs: $29, Stay limit: 14 days, Open all year, Reservations accepted, Elev: 74ft/23m, Tel: 352-369-2693, Nearest town: Ocala. GPS: 29.103759, -82.093316

14 • B4 | Marjorie Harris Carr Cross-Florida Greenway - Shangri-La

Total sites: 24, RV sites: 24, Central water, Flush toilet, Free showers, RV dump, Tents: $18/RVs: $25, Generator hours: 0700-2300, Reservations accepted, Elev: 76ft/23m, Tel: 352-347-1163, Nearest town: Ocala. GPS: 29.038303, -82.239837

Idaho

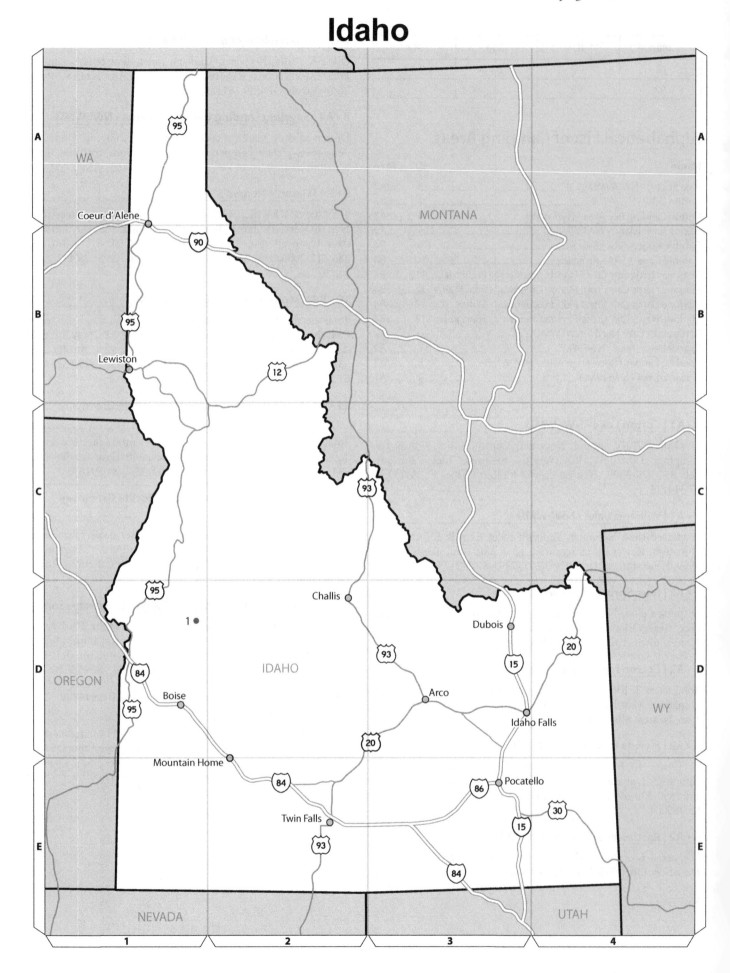

Map	ID	Map	ID
D1	1		

Alphabetical List of Camping Areas

Name   **ID**   **Map**

1 • D1 | Wellington Sno-Park

Dispersed sites, No water, Vault/pit toilet, Tent & RV camping: Free, Elev: 4528ft/1380m, Nearest town: Smiths Ferry. GPS: 44.297534, -116.088821

Illinois

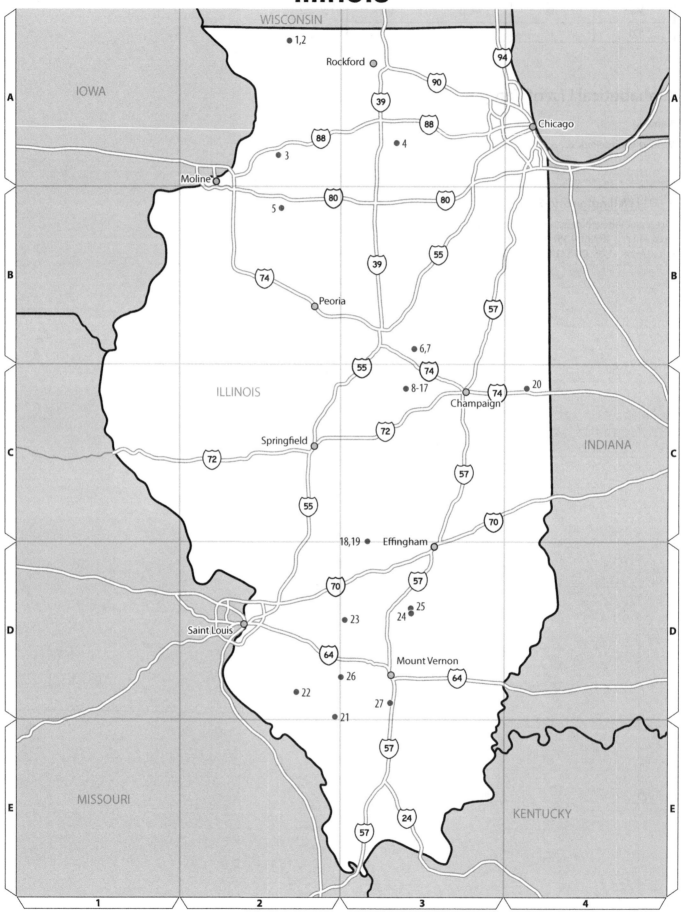

Map	ID	Map	ID
A2	1-3	C3	8-19
A3	4	C4	20
B2	5	D2	21-22
B3	6-7	D3	23-27

Alphabetical List of Camping Areas

1 • A2 | Lake-Le-Aqua-Na SRA - Buck Hollow Equestrian

Dispersed sites, Central water, Vault/pit toilet, Tent & RV camping: $20, Stay limit: 14 days, Open all year, Reservations not accepted, Elev: 971ft/296m, Tel: 815-369-4282, Nearest town: Lena. GPS: 42.418223, -89.838401

2 • A2 | Lake-Le-Aqua-Na SRA - Hickory Hill

Total sites: 138, RV sites: 108, Elec sites: 108, Central water, Flush toilet, Free showers, RV dump, Tents: $10/RVs: $20-30, No water in winter, Stay limit: 14 days, Open all year, Max Length: 40ft, Reservations accepted, Elev: 922ft/281m, Tel: 815-369-4282, Nearest town: Lena. GPS: 42.424377, -89.837347

3 • A2 | Prophetstown SRA

Total sites: 43+, RV sites: 43+, Elec sites: 43+, Central water, Flush toilet, Free showers, RV dump, Tent & RV camping: $20-30, Stay limit: 14 days, Open May-Oct, Reservations accepted, Elev: 617ft/ 188m, Tel: 815-537-2926, Nearest town: Prophetstown. GPS: 41.672119, -89.925537

4 • A3 | Shabbona Lake SRA

Total sites: 150, RV sites: 150, Elec sites: 150, Central water, Flush toilet, Free showers, RV dump, Tent & RV camping: $20-30, Stay limit: 14 days, Open all year, Max Length: 40ft, Elev: 889ft/271m, Tel: 815-824-2106, Nearest town: Shabbona. GPS: 41.751428, -88.869906

5 • B2 | Johnson-Sauk Trail SRA

Total sites: 95, RV sites: 70, Elec sites: 70, Central water, Flush toilet, Free showers, RV dump, Tents: $8/RVs: $20-30, No water Nov-Apr, Stay limit: 14 days, Open all year, Reservations accepted, Elev: 784ft/239m, Tel: 309-853-5589, Nearest town: Kewanee. GPS: 41.325275, -89.891105

6 • B3 | Moraine View SRA - Gander Bay

Total sites: 102, RV sites: 102, Elec sites: 137, Central water, Flush toilet, Free showers, RV dump, Tent & RV camping: $20-30, $30 on holiday weekends, Stay limit: 14 days, Open all year, Max Length: 35ft, Reservations accepted, Elev: 856ft/261m, Tel: 309-724-8032, Nearest town: LeRoy. GPS: 40.415915, -88.719965

7 • B3 | Moraine View SRA - Timberline Ridge Equestrian

Total sites: 30, RV sites: 30, Elec sites: 30, Water at site, Flush toilet, Free showers, No RV dump, Tent & RV camping: $20-30, $30 on holiday weekends, Stay limit: 14 days, Open all year, Elev: 863ft/ 263m, Tel: 309-724-8032, Nearest town: LeRoy. GPS: 40.415756, -88.731761

8 • C3 | Clinton Lake SRA - Loop A

Total sites: 52, RV sites: 52, Elec sites: 52, Central water, Flush toilet, Free showers, RV dump, Tent & RV camping: $20-30, Bathhouses closed Nov-Apr, Stay limit: 14 days, Open all year, Max Length: 40ft, Reservations accepted, Elev: 729ft/222m, Tel: 217-935-8722, Nearest town: DeWitt. GPS: 40.160931, -88.790776

9 • C3 | Clinton Lake SRA - Loop B

Total sites: 41, RV sites: 41, Elec sites: 33, Central water, Flush toilet, Free showers, RV dump, Tents: $12/RVs: $20-30, Bathhouses closed Nov-Apr, Stay limit: 14 days, Open all year, Max Length: 40ft, Reservations accepted, Elev: 734ft/224m, Tel: 217-935-8722, Nearest town: DeWitt. GPS: 40.162033, -88.795364

10 • C3 | Clinton Lake SRA - Loop C

Total sites: 20, RV sites: 20, Elec sites: 20, Central water, Flush toilet, Free showers, RV dump, Tent & RV camping: $20-30, Bathhouses closed Nov-Apr, Stay limit: 14 days, Open all year, Max Length: 40ft, Reservations accepted, Elev: 735ft/224m, Tel: 217-935-8722, Nearest town: DeWitt. GPS: 40.161689, -88.797106

11 • C3 | Clinton Lake SRA - Loop D

Total sites: 42, RV sites: 42, Elec sites: 42, Central water, Flush toilet, Free showers, RV dump, Tent & RV camping: $20-30, Bathhouses closed Nov-Apr, Stay limit: 14 days, Open all year, Max Length: 40ft, Reservations accepted, Elev: 734ft/224m, Tel: 217-935-8722, Nearest town: DeWitt. GPS: 40.160935, -88.798125

12 • C3 | Clinton Lake SRA - Loop E

Total sites: 18, RV sites: 18, Elec sites: 18, Central water, Flush toilet, Free showers, RV dump, Tent & RV camping: $20-30, Bathhouses closed Nov-Apr, Stay limit: 14 days, Open all year, Max Length: 40ft, Reservations accepted, Elev: 731ft/223m, Tel: 217-935-8722, Nearest town: DeWitt. GPS: 40.156635, -88.799446

13 • C3 | Clinton Lake SRA - Loop F

Total sites: 22, RV sites: 22, Elec sites: 22, Central water, Flush toilet, Free showers, RV dump, Tent & RV camping: $20-30, Bathhouses closed Nov-Apr, Stay limit: 14 days, Open all year, Max Length: 40ft, Reservations accepted, Elev: 731ft/223m, Tel: 217-935-8722, Nearest town: DeWitt. GPS: 40.155962, -88.796263

14 • C3 | Clinton Lake SRA - Loop G

Total sites: 33, RV sites: 33, Elec sites: 33, Central water, Flush toilet, Free showers, RV dump, Tent & RV camping: $20-30, Bathhouses closed Nov-Apr, Stay limit: 14 days, Open all year, Max Length: 40ft, Reservations accepted, Elev: 730ft/223m, Tel: 217-935-8722, Nearest town: DeWitt. GPS: 40.155083, -88.797913

15 • C3 | Clinton Lake SRA - Loop H

Total sites: 26, RV sites: 26, Elec sites: 26, Central water, Flush toilet, Free showers, RV dump, Tent & RV camping: $20-30, Bathhouses closed Nov-Apr, Stay limit: 14 days, Open all year, Max Length: 40ft, Reservations accepted, Elev: 731ft/223m, Tel: 217-935-8722, Nearest town: DeWitt. GPS: 40.154694, -88.802525

16 • C3 | Clinton Lake SRA - Loop I

Total sites: 32, RV sites: 32, Elec sites: 32, Central water, Flush toilet, Free showers, RV dump, Tent & RV camping: $20-30, Bathhouses closed Nov-Apr, Stay limit: 14 days, Open all year, Max Length: 40ft, Reservations accepted, Elev: 728ft/222m, Tel: 217-935-8722, Nearest town: DeWitt. GPS: 40.153417, -88.801833

17 • C3 | Clinton Lake SRA - Loop J

Total sites: 18, RV sites: 18, Elec sites: 18, Central water, Flush toilet, Free showers, RV dump, Tent & RV camping: $20-30, Bathhouses closed Nov-Apr, Stay limit: 14 days, Open all year, Max Length: 40ft, Reservations accepted, Elev: 725ft/221m, Tel: 217-935-8722, Nearest town: DeWitt. GPS: 40.152476, -88.799994

18 • C3 | Ramsey Lake SRA - Hickory Grove

Total sites: 45, RV sites: 45, Vault/pit toilet, Tent & RV camping: $8, Stay limit: 14 days, Open all year, Reservations not accepted, Elev: 633ft/193m, Tel: 618-423-2215, Nearest town: Ramsey. GPS: 39.164032, -89.126769

19 • C3 | Ramsey Lake SRA - White Oak

Total sites: 90, RV sites: 90, Elec sites: 90, Central water, Flush toilet, Free showers, RV dump, Tent & RV camping: $20-30, $30 on holiday weekends, Stay limit: 14 days, Open all year, Max Length: 70ft, Reservations accepted, Elev: 643ft/196m, Tel: 618-423-2215, Nearest town: Ramsey. GPS: 39.159349, -89.132213

20 • C4 | Kickapoo SRA

Total sites: 184, RV sites: 184, Elec sites: 101, Central water, Flush toilet, Free showers, RV dump, Tents: $8/RVs: $20-30, Stay limit: 14 days, Open all year, Max Length: 40ft, Elev: 646ft/197m, Tel: 217-442-4915, Nearest town: Oakwood. GPS: 40.135756, -87.738245

21 • D2 | Pyramid SRA

Total sites: 79, RV sites: 79, Central water, Vault/pit toilet, No showers, No RV dump, Tent & RV camping: $6-8, Also walk-to sites, Some equestrian sites, Open all year, Reservations not accepted, Elev: 456ft/139m, Tel: 618-357-2574, Nearest town: Pinckneyville. GPS: 38.020332, -89.401886

22 • D2 | World Shooting and Recreational Complex - DNR

Total sites: 1001, RV sites: 1001, Elec sites: 1001, Water at site, RV dump, Tents: $10/RVs: $20-35, Max Length: 50ft, Reservations accepted, Elev: 466ft/142m, Tel: 618-295-2700, Nearest town: Sparta. GPS: 38.184289, -89.730817

23 • D3 | Eldon Hazlet SRA

Total sites: 364, RV sites: 328, Elec sites: 328, Central water, Flush toilet, Free showers, RV dump, Tents: $8/RVs: $20-30, Open all year, Max Length: 45ft, Elev: 472ft/144m, Tel: 618-594-3015, Nearest town: Carlyle. GPS: 38.654553, -89.328157

24 • D3 | Stephen A. Forbes SRA - Equestrian CG

Total sites: 21, RV sites: 21, Elec sites: 21, Water available, Vault/pit toilet, No showers, No RV dump, Tents: $20/RVs: $20-30, Stay limit: 14 days, Open all year, Elev: 545ft/166m, Tel: 618-547-3381, Nearest town: Kinmundy. GPS: 38.705155, -88.761260

25 • D3 | Stephen A. Forbes SRA - Oak Ridge CG

Total sites: 115, RV sites: 115, Elec sites: 115, Water available, Flush toilet, Free showers, RV dump, Tent & RV camping: $20-30, Stay limit: 14 days, Open all year, Max Length: 40ft, Reservations accepted, Elev: 571ft/174m, Tel: 618-547-3381, Nearest town: Kinmundy. GPS: 38.731743, -88.772025

26 • D3 | Washington County SRA - Shady Rest CG

Total sites: 37, RV sites: 37, Elec sites: 37, Central water, Flush toilet, Free showers, RV dump, Tent & RV camping: $20-30, Also cabins, Stay limit: 14 days, Open all year, Max Length: 40ft, Reservations accepted, Elev: 525ft/160m, Tel: 618-327-3137, Nearest town: Nashville. GPS: 38.285333, -89.353823

27 • D3 | Wayne Fitzgerrell SRA - Bay Area

Total sites: 260, RV sites: 243, Elec sites: 243, Central water, Flush toilet, Free showers, RV dump, Tents: $6/RVs: $20-30, Also cabins, Stay limit: 14 days, Max Length: 42ft, Reservations accepted, Elev: 426ft/130m, Tel: 618-629-2320, Nearest town: Whittington. GPS: 38.113146, -88.939747

Indiana

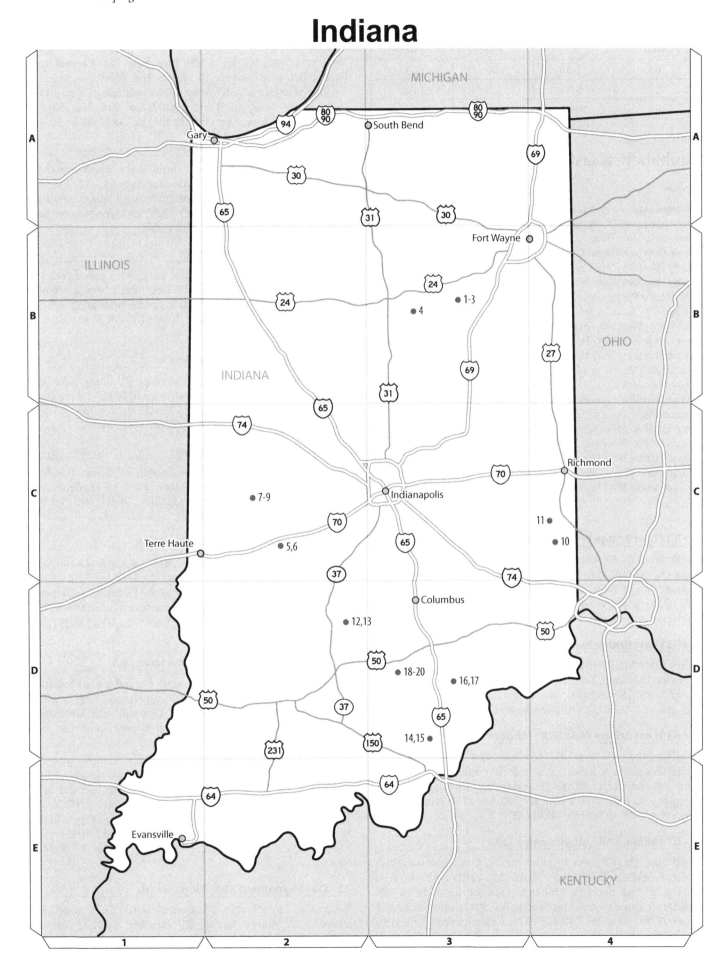

Map	ID	Map	ID
B3	1-4	D2	12-13
C2	5-9	D3	14-20
C4	10-11		

Alphabetical List of Camping Areas

1 • B3 | Lost Bridge West SRA - Apple Orchard

Total sites: 37, RV sites: 37, Central water, Vault/pit toilet, No showers, No RV dump, Tent & RV camping: $12, One-time entrance fee of $9 ($7 IN residents), Open all year, Max Length: 80ft, Reservations accepted, Elev: 817ft/249m, Tel: 260-468-2125, Nearest town: Andrews. GPS: 40.766226, -85.632754

2 • B3 | Lost Bridge West SRA - Horseman's Camp

Total sites: 51, RV sites: 51, Central water, Flush toilet, Free showers, RV dump, Tent & RV camping: $13, One-time entrance fee of $9 ($7 IN residents), Max Length: 120ft, Elev: 814ft/248m, Tel: 260-468-2125. GPS: 40.767968, -85.636013

3 • B3 | Lost Bridge West SRA - Modern

Total sites: 245, RV sites: 245, Elec sites: 245, Central water, Flush toilet, Free showers, RV dump, Tent & RV camping: $23-33, One-time entrance fee of $9 ($7 IN residents), Open all year, Max Length: 65ft, Elev: 810ft/247m, Tel: 260-468-2125, Nearest town: Andrews. GPS: 40.769116, -85.611337

4 • B3 | Miami SRA - Mississinewa Lake

Total sites: 431, RV sites: 431, Elec sites: 374, Water at site, Flush toilet, Free showers, RV dump, Tents: $16-22/RVs: $23-44, Also cabins, 39 Full hookups, One-time entrance fee of $9 ($7 IN residents), Open all year, Max Length: 70ft, Reservations accepted, Elev: 787ft/240m, Tel: 765-473-6528, Nearest town: Peru. GPS: 40.701198, -85.943959

5 • C2 | Lieber SRA - Poplar Grove

Total sites: 120, RV sites: 120, Elec sites: 120, Central water, Flush toilet, Free showers, RV dump, Tent & RV camping: $23-33, One-time entrance fee of $9 ($7 IN residents), Open all year, Reservations accepted, Elev: 846ft/258m, Tel: 765-795-4576, Nearest town: Cloverdale. GPS: 39.483128, -86.878985

6 • C2 | Lieber SRA - Sunny Acres

Total sites: 96, RV sites: 96, Central water, Flush toilet, Free showers, RV dump, Tent & RV camping: $16-22, One-time entrance fee of $9 ($7 IN residents), Open all year, Reservations accepted, Elev: 810ft/247m, Tel: 765-795-4576, Nearest town: Cloverdale. GPS: 39.483498, -86.886508

7 • C2 | Raccoon SRA - Electric

Total sites: 312, RV sites: 277, Elec sites: 240, Central water, RV dump, Tents: $6-10/RVs: $10-27, One-time entrance fee of $9 ($7 IN residents), Max Length: 82ft, Reservations accepted, Elev: 741ft/226m, Tel: 765-344-1412, Nearest town: Rockville. GPS: 39.735331, -87.075571

8 • C2 | Raccoon SRA - Lake-view

Total sites: 40, RV sites: 40, Central water, RV dump, Tent & RV camping: $16-22, One-time entrance fee of $9 ($7 IN residents), Reservations not accepted, Elev: 722ft/220m, Tel: 765-344-1412, Nearest town: Rockville. GPS: 39.733961, -87.081863

9 • C2 | Raccoon SRA - Primitive

Total sites: 35, RV sites: 35, Central water, RV dump, Tent & RV camping: $12, One-time entrance fee of $9 ($7 IN residents), Max Length: 50ft, Reservations accepted, Elev: 743ft/226m, Tel: 765-344-1412, Nearest town: Rockville. GPS: 39.736441, -87.070891

10 • C4 | Brookville Lake - Mounds SRA

Total sites: 269, RV sites: 269, Elec sites: 269, Central water, Flush toilet, Free showers, RV dump, Tents: $23-33/RVs: $23-44, 62 Full hookups, One-time entrance fee of $9 ($7 IN residents), Open all year, Max Length: 66ft, Reservations accepted, Elev: 968ft/295m, Tel: 765-647-2657, Nearest town: Brookville. GPS: 39.494053, -84.964768

11 • C4 | Brookville Lake - Quakertown SRA

Total sites: 97, RV sites: 97, Elec sites: 97, Central water, Flush toilet, Free showers, RV dump, Tent & RV camping: $23-33, One-time entrance fee of $9 ($7 IN residents), Open all year, Reservations accepted, Elev: 866ft/264m, Nearest town: Brookville. GPS: 39.602731, -84.998123

12 • D2 | Paynetown SRA

Total sites: 242, RV sites: 226, Elec sites: 226, Central water, Flush toilet, Free showers, RV dump, Tents: $16-22/RVs: $23-33, One-time entrance fee of $9 ($7 IN residents), Open all year, Max Length: 90ft, Reservations accepted, Elev: 571ft/174m, Tel: 812-837-9546, Nearest town: Bloomington. GPS: 39.080942, -86.437063

13 • D2 | Paynetown SRA - Non-electric

Total sites: 75, RV sites: 75, Central water, Flush toilet, Free showers, RV dump, Tent & RV camping: $16-22, One-time entrance fee of $9 ($7 IN residents), Open all year, Reservations accepted, Elev: 565ft/172m, Tel: 812-837-9546, Nearest town: Bloomington. GPS: 39.083144, -86.434318

14 • D3 | Deam Lake SRA - Family

Total sites: 116, RV sites: 116, Elec sites: 116, Central water, Flush toilet, Free showers, RV dump, Tent & RV camping: $23-33, One-time entrance fee of $9 ($7 IN residents), Open Mar-Nov, Max Length: 65ft, Reservations accepted, Elev: 610ft/186m, Tel: 812-246-5421, Nearest town: Borden. GPS: 38.473261, -85.863997

15 • D3 | Deam Lake SRA - Horse Camp

Total sites: 68, RV sites: 68, Elec sites: 68, Central water, Flush toilet, Free showers, RV dump, Tent & RV camping: $26-36, One-time entrance fee of $9 ($7 IN residents), Open Mar-Nov, Max Length: 65ft, Reservations accepted, Elev: 558ft/170m, Tel: 812-246-5421, Nearest town: Borden. GPS: 38.474533, -85.860407

16 • D3 | Hardy Lake SRA - Shale Bluff

Total sites: 149, RV sites: 149, Elec sites: 149, Central water, Flush toilet, Free showers, RV dump, Tent & RV camping: $23-33, One-time entrance fee of $9 ($7 IN residents), Open all year, Max Length: 50ft, Reservations accepted, Elev: 650ft/198m, Tel: 812-794-3800, Nearest town: Austin. GPS: 38.776363, -85.692584

17 • D3 | Hardy Lake SRA - Wooster Primitive

Total sites: 18, RV sites: 18, Central water, Vault/pit toilet, No showers, No RV dump, Tent & RV camping: $12, One-time entrance fee of $9 ($7 IN residents), Reservations accepted, Elev: 636ft/194m, Tel: 812-794-3800, Nearest town: Scottsburg. GPS: 38.772881, -85.692070

18 • D3 | Starve-Hollow SRA - Electric

Total sites: 90, RV sites: 90, Elec sites: 90, Flush toilet, Free showers, RV dump, Tent & RV camping: $23-33, One-time entrance fee of $9 ($7 IN residents), Max Length: 35ft, Reservations accepted, Elev: 552ft/168m, Tel: 812-358-3464, Nearest town: Vallonia. GPS: 38.816650, -86.076660

19 • D3 | Starve-Hollow SRA - FHU

Total sites: 53, RV sites: 53, Elec sites: 53, Water at site, Flush toilet, Free showers, RV dump, No tents/RVs: $30-44, 53 Full hookups, One-time entrance fee of $9 ($7 IN residents), Max Length: 35ft, Reservations accepted, Elev: 572ft/174m, Tel: 812-358-3464, Nearest town: Vallonia. GPS: 38.817576, -86.080465

20 • D3 | Starve-Hollow SRA - Non-electric

Total sites: 10, RV sites: 10, Flush toilet, Free showers, RV dump, Tent & RV camping: $16-22, One-time entrance fee of $9 ($7 IN residents), Elev: 557ft/170m, Tel: 812-358-3464, Nearest town: Vallonia. GPS: 38.819512, -86.075595

Iowa

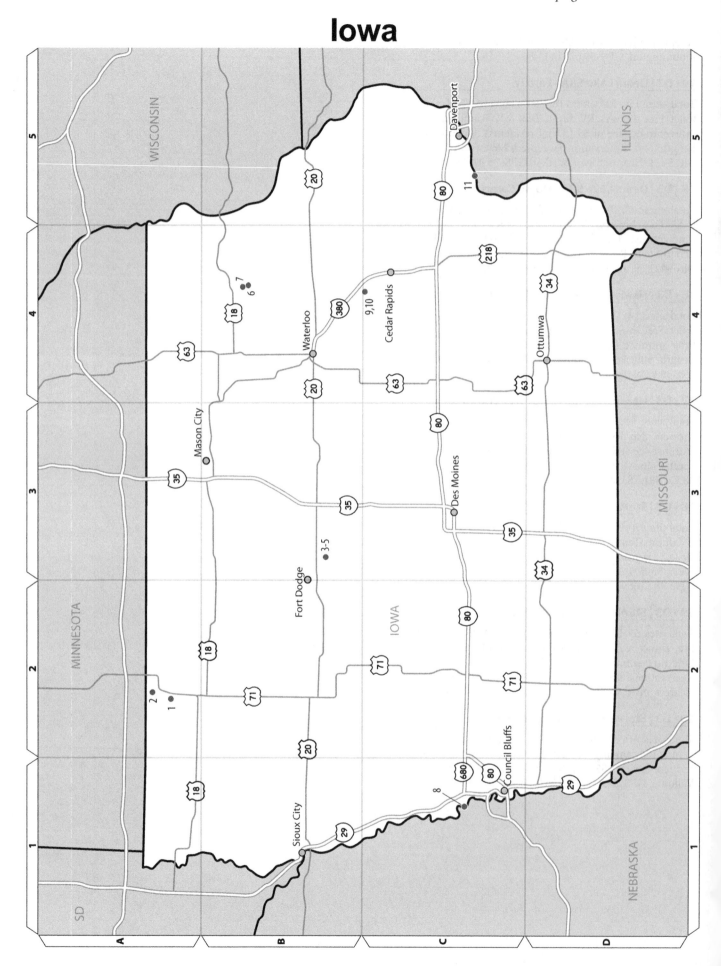

Map	ID	Map	ID
A2	1-2	C1	8
B3	3-5	C4	9-10
B4	6-7	C5	11

Alphabetical List of Camping Areas

1 • A2 | Emerson Bay SRA

Total sites: 82, RV sites: 82, Elec sites: 82, Water at site, Flush toilet, Free showers, RV dump, Tent & RV camping: $12-26, 24 Full hookups, Open all year, Max Length: 110ft, Reservations accepted, Elev: 1388ft/423m, Tel: 712-337-3211, Nearest town: West Okoboji. GPS: 43.355225, -95.174561

2 • A2 | Marble Beach SRA

Total sites: 122, RV sites: 82, Elec sites: 94, Central water, Flush toilet, Free showers, RV dump, Tents: $6-20/RVs: $12-26, 68 Full hookups, Open all year, Max Length: 100ft, Reservations accepted, Elev: 1404ft/428m, Tel: 712-337-3211, Nearest town: Milford. GPS: 43.469482, -95.124756

3 • B3 | Brushy Creek SRA - Beach CG

Total sites: 47, RV sites: 47, Elec sites: 47, Water at site, Flush toilet, Free showers, RV dump, Tent & RV camping: $12-26, 8 Full hookups, Open all year, Max Length: 104ft, Reservations accepted, Elev: 1086ft/331m, Tel: 515-543-8298, Nearest town: Lehigh. GPS: 42.389876, -93.989095

4 • B3 | Brushy Creek SRA - North Equestrian CG

Total sites: 125, RV sites: 125, Elec sites: 50, Central water, Flush toilet, Free showers, Tent & RV camping: $10-26, 1 Full hookups, Open all year, Max Length: 113ft, Reservations accepted, Elev: 1102ft/336m, Tel: 515-543-8298, Nearest town: Lehigh. GPS: 42.402012, -93.995366

5 • B3 | Brushy Creek SRA - South Equestrian CG

Total sites: 92, RV sites: 92, Elec sites: 70, Water at site, Flush toilet, Free showers, Tent & RV camping: $10-26, 8 Full hookups, Open all year, Max Length: 113ft, Reservations accepted, Elev: 1083ft/330m, Tel: 515-543-8298, Nearest town: Lehigh. GPS: 42.368369, -93.984829

6 • B4 | Volga River SRA - Albany

Total sites: 44, RV sites: 34, Elec sites: 34, Central water, Vault/pit toilet, No showers, No RV dump, Tents: $12-21/RVs: $16-22, 34 equestrian sites, Open all year, Reservations accepted, Elev: 935ft/285m, Tel: 563-425-4161, Nearest town: Fayette. GPS: 42.864372, -91.757421

7 • B4 | Volga River SRA - Lakeview

Total sites: 41, RV sites: 41, Elec sites: 41, Water at site, Flush toilet, Free showers, RV dump, Tent & RV camping: $12-24, 35 Full hookups, Youth group site: $15, Open all year, Max Length: 90ft, Reservations accepted, Elev: 1096ft/334m, Tel: 563-425-4161, Nearest town: Fayette. GPS: 42.898081, -91.763117

8 • C1 | Wilson Island SRA

Total sites: 42, RV sites: 42, Elec sites: 32, Central water, Flush toilet, Free showers, RV dump, Tents: $6-14/RVs: $12-20, Also cabins, Open Apr-Oct, Max Length: 70ft, Reservations accepted, Elev: 1001ft/305m, Tel: 712-642-2069, Nearest town: Missouri Valley. GPS: 41.484081, -96.013232

9 • C4 | Pleasant Creek SRA - CG 1

Total sites: 27, RV sites: 27, Elec sites: 27, Water at site, Flush toilet, Free showers, RV dump, Tents: $12-20/RVs: $12-26, 1 Full hookups, 30A only, Reservations accepted, Elev: 873ft/266m, Tel: 319-436-7716, Nearest town: Palo. GPS: 42.129887, -91.822699

10 • C4 | Pleasant Creek SRA - CG 2

Total sites: 30, RV sites: 30, Elec sites: 30, Central water, Flush toilet, Free showers, RV dump, Tent & RV camping: $12-20, Also cabins, 50A, Max Length: 110ft, Reservations accepted, Elev: 866ft/264m, Tel: 319-436-7716, Nearest town: Palo. GPS: 42.131675, -91.827435

11 • C5 | Fairport SRA

Total sites: 42, RV sites: 42, Elec sites: 42, Central water, Flush toilet, Free showers, RV dump, Tent & RV camping: $12-18, Open all year, Max Length: 50ft, Reservations accepted, Elev: 577ft/176m, Tel: 563-263-4337, Nearest town: Muscatine. GPS: 41.432367, -90.924639

Kentucky

WEST VIRGINIA

VIRGINIA

NORTH CAROLINA

OHIO

Prestonsburg

Jackson

Maysville

Corbin

75

Lexington

75

75

64

Harrodsburg

Campbellsville

KENTUCKY

71

65

Louisville

1

Bowling Green

65

INDIANA

Madisonville

Hopkinsville

24

Paducah

MO

ILLINOIS

TENNESSEE

5

4

3

2

1

A

B

C

D

Map	ID	Map	ID
B3	1		

Alphabetical List of Camping Areas

Name   **ID**   **Map**

Otter Creek Outdoor Rec Area - DFWR...1 .... B3

1 • B3 | Otter Creek Outdoor Rec Area - DFWR

Total sites: 143, RV sites: 77, Elec sites: 77, Water at site, Flush toilet, Free showers, RV dump, Tents: $12/RVs: $15-22, Also cabins, Stay limit: 30 days, Open all year, Reservations accepted, Elev: 647ft/197m, Tel: 502-924-9171, Nearest town: Brandenburg. GPS: 37.945303, -86.050083

Louisiana

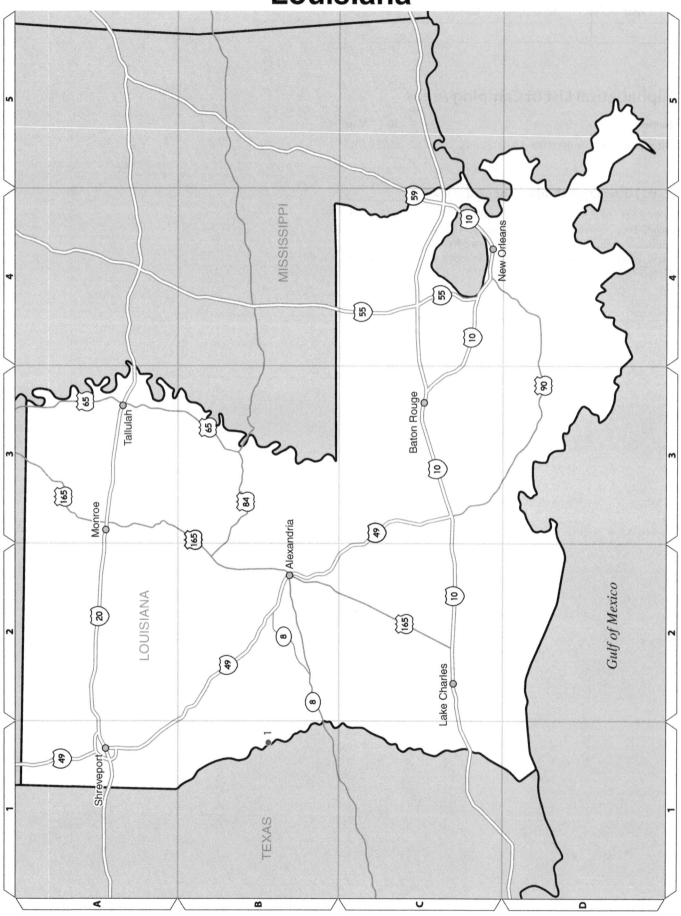

Map	ID	Map	ID
B1	1		

Alphabetical List of Camping Areas

Name	ID	Map
Cypress Bend - SRA	1	B1

1 • B1 | Cypress Bend - SRA

Total sites: 95, RV sites: 60, Elec sites: 60, Water at site, Flush toilet, Free showers, RV dump, Tent & RV camping: $25-35, 60 Full hookups, Open all year, Reservations accepted, Elev: 272ft/ 83m, Tel: 318-256-4112, Nearest town: Many. GPS: 31.421036, -93.676669

Maine

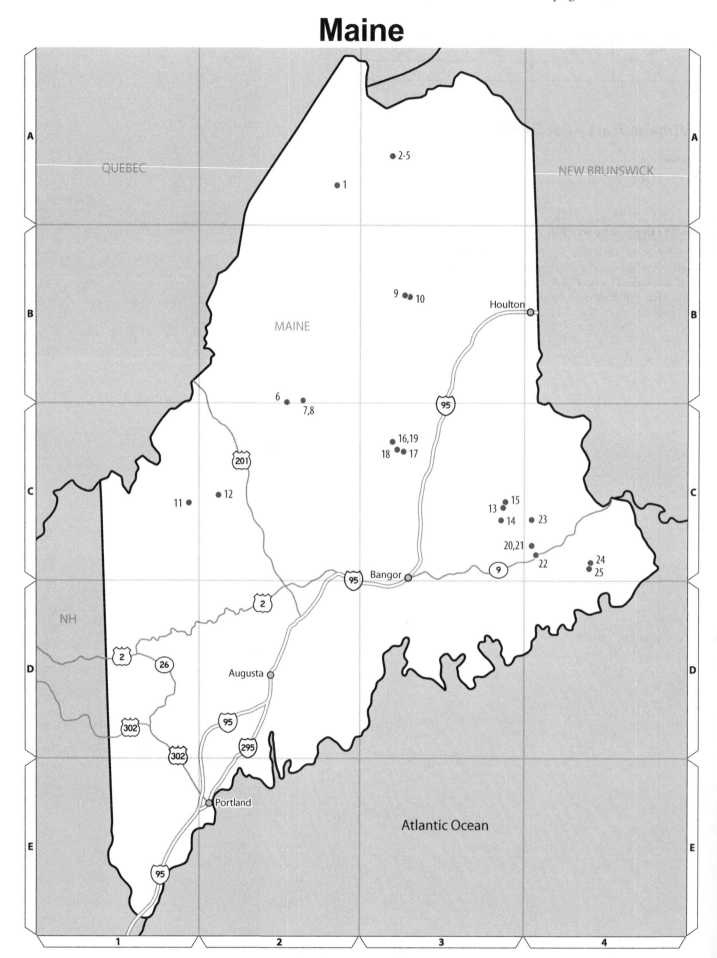

Map	ID	Map	ID
A2	1	C1	11
A3	2-5	C2	12
B2	6-8	C3	13-19
B3	9-10	C4	20-25

Alphabetical List of Camping Areas

Name	ID	Map
Big Eddy - Dead River PRL	12	C2
Bigelow Preserve PRL	11	C1
Deboullie PRL - Deboullie East	2	A3
Deboullie PRL - Denny Pond	3	A3
Deboullie PRL - Pushineer Pond	4	A3
Deboullie PRL - Togue Pond	5	A3
Duck Lake PRL - Duck Lake	13	C3
Duck Lake PRL - Gassabias Lake	14	C3
Duck Lake PRL - Middle Unknown Lake	15	C3
Machias River Corridor PRL - River Rd #1	20	C4
Machias River Corridor PRL - River Rd #2	21	C4
Machias River Corridor PRL - Rt 9	22	C4
Machias River Corridor PRL - Third Machias Lake	23	C4
Moosehead Lake PRL - Cowan West	6	B2
Moosehead Lake PRL - Spencer Bay	7	B2
Moosehead Lake PRL - Spencer Bay North	8	B2
Rocky Lake PRL - Mud Landing	24	C4
Rocky Lake PRL - South Bay	25	C4
Round Pond PRL	1	A2
Scraggly Lake PRL - Green Pond	9	B3
Scraggly Lake PRL - Scraggly Lake	10	B3
Seboeis PRL - Boat Landing	16	C3
Seboeis PRL - Endless Outlet	17	C3
Seboeis PRL - Seboeis Outlet	18	C3
Seboeis PRL - The Pit	19	C3

1 • A2 | Round Pond PRL

Dispersed sites, No water, No toilets, Tent & RV camping: Free, Reservations not accepted, Elev: 1234ft/376m, Tel: 207-435-7963, Nearest town: Allagash. GPS: 46.802801, -69.290549

2 • A3 | Deboullie PRL - Deboullie East

Dispersed sites, No water, No toilets, Tent & RV camping: Free, Reservations not accepted, Elev: 1158ft/353m, Tel: 207-435-7963, Nearest town: St. Francis. GPS: 46.964425, -68.838583

3 • A3 | Deboullie PRL - Denny Pond

Dispersed sites, No water, No toilets, Tent & RV camping: Free, Reservations not accepted, Elev: 1332ft/406m, Tel: 207-435-7963, Nearest town: St. Francis. GPS: 46.943367, -68.869021

4 • A3 | Deboullie PRL - Pushineer Pond

Dispersed sites, No toilets, Tent & RV camping: Free, Reservations not accepted, Elev: 1132ft/345m, Tel: 207-435-7963, Nearest town: St. Francis. GPS: 46.958942, -68.837961

5 • A3 | Deboullie PRL - Togue Pond

Dispersed sites, No toilets, Tent & RV camping: Free, Reservations not accepted, Elev: 1280ft/390m, Tel: 207-435-7963, Nearest town: St. Francis. GPS: 46.934651, -68.880605

6 • B2 | Moosehead Lake PRL - Cowan West

Total sites: 18, RV sites: 10, No water, Vault/pit toilet, Tent & RV camping: Free, Reservations not accepted, Elev: 1028ft/313m, Tel: 207-778-8231, Nearest town: Greenville. GPS: 45.700831, -69.683713

7 • B2 | Moosehead Lake PRL - Spencer Bay

Total sites: 35, RV sites: 35, No water, Vault/pit toilet, Tent & RV camping: Free, Reservations not accepted, Elev: 1040ft/317m, Tel: 207-778-8231, Nearest town: Greenville. GPS: 45.710072, -69.555465

8 • B2 | Moosehead Lake PRL - Spencer Bay North

Total sites: 5, No water, Vault/pit toilet, Tent & RV camping: Free, Reservations not accepted, Elev: 1038ft/316m, Tel: 207-778-8231, Nearest town: Greenville. GPS: 45.714439, -69.558301

9 • B3 | Scraggly Lake PRL - Green Pond

Dispersed sites, No water, No toilets, Tent & RV camping: Free, Reservations not accepted, Elev: 742ft/226m, Tel: 207-435-7963, Nearest town: Moosehorn Crossing. GPS: 46.239831, -68.790009

10 • B3 | Scraggly Lake PRL - Scraggly Lake

Total sites: 12, No water, No toilets, Tent & RV camping: Free, Reservations not accepted, Elev: 722ft/220m, Tel: 207-435-7963, Nearest town: Moosehorn Crossing. GPS: 46.230222, -68.744644

11 • C1 | Bigelow Preserve PRL

Dispersed sites, No water, No toilets, Tent & RV camping: Free, Open all year, Reservations not accepted, Elev: 1138ft/347m, Tel: 207-778-8231, Nearest town: Stratton. GPS: 45.188826, -70.415013

12 • C2 | Big Eddy - Dead River PRL

Total sites: 14, RV sites: 10, No water, No toilets, Tent & RV camping: Free, Open all year, Reservations not accepted, Elev: 1060ft/323m, Tel: 207-778-8231, Nearest town: Eustis. GPS: 45.230906, -70.195416

13 • C3 | Duck Lake PRL - Duck Lake

Total sites: 10, RV sites: 10, No water, No toilets, Tent & RV camping: Free, Open all year, Reservations not accepted, Elev: 548ft/167m, Tel: 207-941-4412, Nearest town: Lincoln. GPS: 45.150558, -68.072283

14 • C3 | Duck Lake PRL - Gassabias Lake

Total sites: 3, RV sites: 3, No water, No toilets, Tent & RV camping: Free, Open all year, Reservations not accepted, Elev: 358ft/109m, Tel: 207-941-4412, Nearest town: Hancock. GPS: 45.087549, -68.085789

15 • C3 | Duck Lake PRL - Middle Unknown Lake

Total sites: 8, No water, No toilets, Tent & RV camping: Free, Open all year, Reservations not accepted, Elev: 358ft/109m, Tel: 207-941-4412, Nearest town: Lincoln. GPS: 45.177159, -68.061501

16 • C3 | Seboeis PRL - Boat Landing

Total sites: 2, RV sites: 2, No water, No toilets, Tent & RV camping: Free, Open all year, Reservations not accepted, Elev: 436ft/133m, Tel: 207-941-4412, Nearest town: Millinocket. GPS: 45.499478, -68.887501

17 • C3 | Seboeis PRL - Endless Outlet

Dispersed sites, No water, No toilets, Tent & RV camping: Free, Open all year, Reservations not accepted, Elev: 436ft/133m, Tel: 207-941-4412, Nearest town: Millinocket. GPS: 45.443918, -68.805329

18 • C3 | Seboeis PRL - Seboeis Outlet

Dispersed sites, No water, No toilets, Tent & RV camping: Free, Open all year, Reservations not accepted, Elev: 472ft/144m, Tel: 207-941-4412, Nearest town: Millinocket. GPS: 45.453537, -68.851214

19 • C3 | Seboeis PRL - The Pit

Dispersed sites, No water, No toilets, Tent & RV camping: Free, Open all year, Reservations not accepted, Elev: 446ft/136m, Tel: 207-941-4412, Nearest town: Millinocket. GPS: 45.500988, -68.888986

20 • C4 | Machias River Corridor PRL - River Rd #1

Total sites: 10, RV sites: 10, No water, No toilets, Tent & RV camping: Free, Open May-Nov, Reservations not accepted, Elev: 223ft/68m, Tel: 207-941-4412, Nearest town: Beddington. GPS: 44.952328, -67.865213

21 • C4 | Machias River Corridor PRL - River Rd #2

Total sites: 2, RV sites: 2, No water, No toilets, Tent & RV camping: Free, Open May-Nov, Reservations not accepted, Elev: 236ft/72m, Tel: 207-941-4412, Nearest town: Beddington. GPS: 44.959115, -67.873061

22 • C4 | Machias River Corridor PRL - Rt 9

Total sites: 6, RV sites: 2, No water, No toilets, Tent & RV camping: Free, Open May-Nov, Reservations not accepted, Elev: 210ft/64m, Tel: 207-941-4412, Nearest town: Beddington. GPS: 44.905909, -67.836219

23 • C4 | Machias River Corridor PRL - Third Machias Lake

Dispersed sites, No water, No toilets, Tent & RV camping: Free, Open May-Nov, Reservations not accepted, Elev: 335ft/102m, Tel: 207-941-4412, Nearest town: Beddington. GPS: 45.089601, -67.863328

24 • C4 | Rocky Lake PRL - Mud Landing

Dispersed sites, No water, No toilets, Tent & RV camping: Free, Reservations not accepted, Elev: 69ft/21m, Tel: 207-941-4412, Nearest town: East Machias. GPS: 44.858911, -67.437691

25 • C4 | Rocky Lake PRL - South Bay

Total sites: 4, RV sites: 2, No water, No toilets, Tent & RV camping: Free, Reservations not accepted, Elev: 59ft/18m, Tel: 207-941-4412, Nearest town: East Machias. GPS: 44.835867, -67.445432

Massachusetts

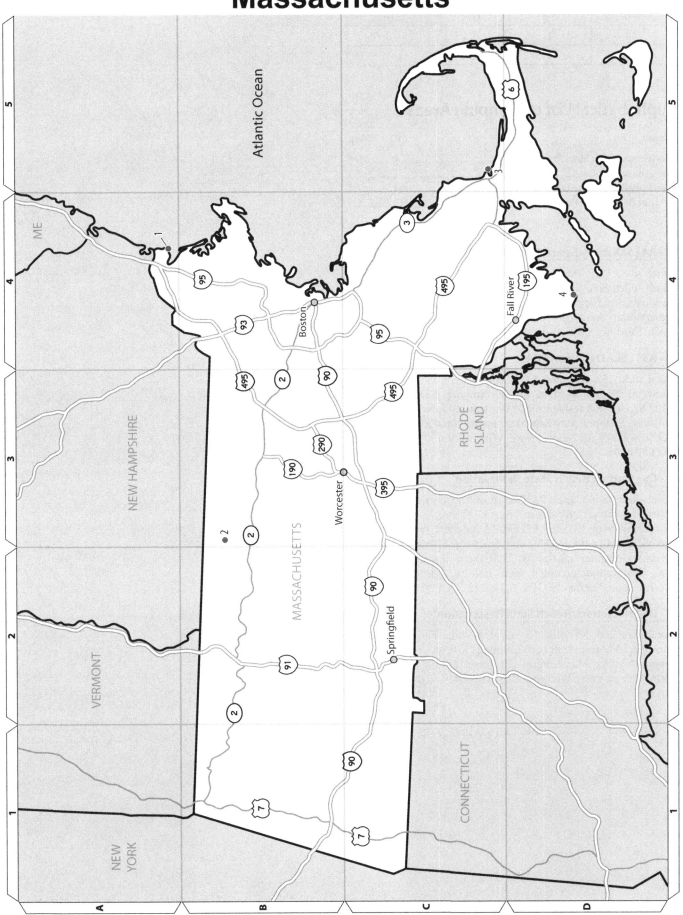

Map	ID	Map	ID
A4	1	C5	3
B3	2	D4	4

Alphabetical List of Camping Areas

1 • A4 | Salisbury Beach State Reservation

Total sites: 452, RV sites: 410, Elec sites: 410, Central water, Flush toilet, Free showers, Tents: $70/RVs: $70-83, $22 for MA residents, Surcharge: $3/night, Open Apr-Nov, Max Length: 40ft, Reservations accepted, Elev: 10ft/3m, Tel: 978-462-4481, Nearest town: Salisbury. GPS: 42.826660, -70.818359

2 • B3 | Lake Dennison SRA

Total sites: 152, RV sites: 147, Central water, Flush toilet, Free showers, RV dump, Tent & RV camping: $54, Group site: $100/$35 for MA residents, MA residents: $17, No pets, Register at Erving SF, Open May-Sep, Max Length: 40ft, Elev: 882ft/269m, Tel: 978-939-8962, Nearest town: Winchendon. GPS: 42.647949, -72.083496

3 • C5 | Scusset Beach State Reservation

Total sites: 97, RV sites: 92, Elec sites: 92, Central water, Flush toilet, Free showers, RV dump, Tents: $70/RVs: $70-82, Campfires not permitted on RV sites, $22 for MA residents, From Nov-Mar: No water/self-contained RVs only, Surcharge $2/night, Stay limit: 14 days, Generator hours: 0700-2200, Open all year, Max Length: 40ft, Reservations accepted, Elev: 10ft/3m, Tel: 508-888-0859, Nearest town: Sandwich. GPS: 41.778320, -70.499756

4 • D4 | Horseneck Beach State Reservation

Total sites: 100, RV sites: 100, Central water, Flush toilet, Free showers, RV dump, Tent & RV camping: $70, MA residents: $22, Open May-Oct, Max Length: 42ft, Elev: 16ft/5m, Tel: 508-636-8816, Nearest town: Westport. GPS: 41.500419, -71.041008

Michigan

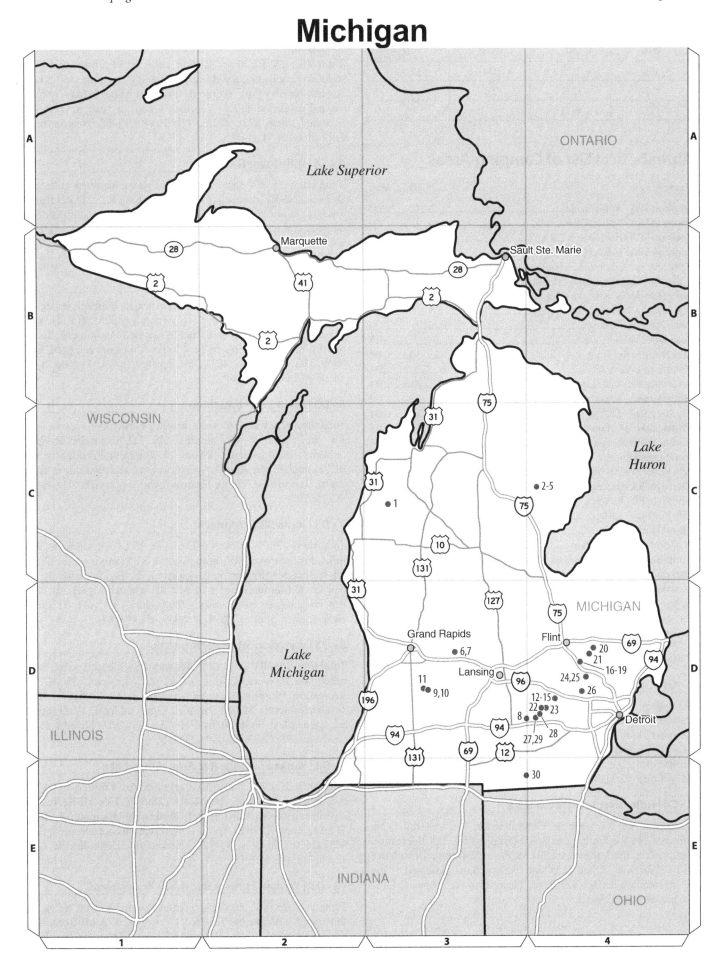

Map	ID	Map	ID
C3	1	D4	12-29
C4	2-5	E3	30
D3	6-11		

Alphabetical List of Camping Areas

1 • C3 | Tippy Dam Rec Area

Total sites: 40, RV sites: 40, Central water, Vault/pit toilet, No showers, No RV dump, Tent & RV camping: $20, MI Recreation Passport required -non-residents: $9/day or $34/annual/residents: $12-$17/annual, Open all year, Reservations accepted, Elev: 715ft/218m, Tel: 800-447-2757, Nearest town: Bretheren. GPS: 44.260653, -85.941827

2 • C4 | Rifle River RA - Devoe Lake

Total sites: 58, RV sites: 58, Central water, Vault/pit toilet, No showers, No RV dump, Tent & RV camping: $20, MI Recreation Passport required -non-residents: $9/day or $34/annual/residents: $12-$17/annual, Open Apr-Nov, Reservations accepted, Elev: 873ft/266m, Tel: 989-473-2258, Nearest town: Lupton. GPS: 44.398369, -84.028682

3 • C4 | Rifle River RA - Grousehaven

Total sites: 75, RV sites: 75, Elec sites: 75, Central water, Flush toilet, Free showers, RV dump, Tent & RV camping: $30-33, MI Recreation Passport required -non-residents: $9/day or $34/annual/residents: $12-$17/annual, Open all year, Reservations accepted, Elev: 892ft/272m, Tel: 989-473-2258, Nearest town: Lupton. GPS: 44.414804, -84.024653

4 • C4 | Rifle River RA - Ranch

Total sites: 25, RV sites: 25, Central water, Vault/pit toilet, No showers, No RV dump, Tent & RV camping: $20, MI Recreation Passport required -non-residents: $9/day or $34/annual/residents: $12-$17/annual, Open all year, Reservations not accepted, Elev: 879ft/268m, Tel: 989-473-2258, Nearest town: Lupton. GPS: 44.391597, -84.036442

5 • C4 | Rifle River RA - Spruce

Total sites: 16, RV sites: 16, Central water, Vault/pit toilet, No showers, No RV dump, Tent & RV camping: $20, MI Recreation Passport required -non-residents: $9/day or $34/annual/residents: $12-$17/annual, Open Apr-Nov, Reservations not accepted, Elev: 886ft/270m, Tel: 989-473-2258, Nearest town: Lupton. GPS: 44.387975, -84.033564

6 • D3 | Ionia SRA - Equestrian

Total sites: 47, RV sites: 47, Central water, Flush toilet, Free showers, RV dump, Tent & RV camping: $20, MI Recreation Passport required -non-residents: $9/day or $34/annual/residents: $12-$17/annual, Open Apr-Oct, Reservations accepted, Elev: 808ft/246m, Tel: 616-527-3750, Nearest town: Ionia. GPS: 42.940875, -85.116705

7 • D3 | Ionia SRA - Modern

Total sites: 100, RV sites: 100, Elec sites: 100, Central water, Flush toilet, Free showers, RV dump, Tent & RV camping: $22-27, $20 off-season, MI Recreation Passport required -non-residents: $9/day or $34/annual/residents: $12-$17/annual, Open Apr-Nov, Reservations accepted, Elev: 789ft/240m, Tel: 616-527-3750, Nearest town: Ionia. GPS: 42.938965, -85.118767

8 • D3 | Waterloo SRA - Portage Lake

Total sites: 136, RV sites: 136, Elec sites: 136, Central water, Flush toilet, Free showers, RV dump, Tent & RV camping: $22-37, MI Recreation Passport required -non-residents: $9/day or $34/annual/residents: $12-$17/annual, Open all year, Reservations accepted, Elev: 988ft/301m, Tel: 734-475-8307, Nearest town: Chelsea. GPS: 42.330380, -84.239920

9 • D3 | Yankee Springs Rec Area - Deep Lake

Total sites: 120, RV sites: 120, Central water, Vault/pit toilet, No showers, No RV dump, Tent & RV camping: $25, MI Recreation Passport required -non-residents: $9/day or $34/annual/residents: $12-$17/annual, Open Apr-Nov, Reservations not accepted, Elev: 863ft/263m, Tel: 269-795-9081, Nearest town: Middleville. GPS: 42.617334, -85.452987

10 • D3 | Yankee Springs Rec Area - Equestrian

Total sites: 25, RV sites: 25, Central water, Vault/pit toilet, No showers, No RV dump, Tent & RV camping: $20, MI Recreation Passport required -non-residents: $9/day or $34/annual/residents:

$12-$17/annual, Open Apr-Nov, Reservations not accepted, Elev: 863ft/263m, Tel: 269-795-9081, Nearest town: Middleville. GPS: 42.600777, -85.472505

11 • D3 | Yankee Springs Rec Area - Gun Lake

Total sites: 197, RV sites: 197, Elec sites: 197, Central water, Flush toilet, Free showers, RV dump, Tent & RV camping: $22-33, MI Recreation Passport required -non-residents: $9/day or $34/annual/residents: $12-$17/annual, Open Apr-Nov, Reservations accepted, Elev: 761ft/232m, Tel: 269-795-9081, Nearest town: Middleville. GPS: 42.615929, -85.515848

12 • D4 | Brighton SRA - Appleton Lake

Total sites: 25, RV sites: 25, Central water, Vault/pit toilet, No showers, No RV dump, Tent & RV camping: $20, MI Recreation Passport required -non-residents: $9/day or $34/annual/residents: $12-$17/annual, Open Apr-Oct, Reservations accepted, Elev: 922ft/281m, Tel: 810-229-6566, Nearest town: Brighton. GPS: 42.506699, -83.834872

13 • D4 | Brighton SRA - Bishop Lake

Total sites: 144, RV sites: 144, Elec sites: 144, Central water, Flush toilet, Free showers, RV dump, Tent & RV camping: $27-30, MI Recreation Passport required -non-residents: $9/day or $34/annual/residents: $12-$17/annual, Open all year, Reservations accepted, Elev: 922ft/281m, Tel: 810-229-6566, Nearest town: Brighton. GPS: 42.501970, -83.845520

14 • D4 | Brighton SRA - Horseman's Camp

Total sites: 19, RV sites: 19, Central water, Vault/pit toilet, No showers, No RV dump, Tent & RV camping: $20, MI Recreation Passport required -non-residents: $9/day or $34/annual/residents: $12-$17/annual, Open Apr-Oct, Reservations accepted, Elev: 981ft/299m, Tel: 810-229-6566, Nearest town: Brighton. GPS: 42.505538, -83.867798

15 • D4 | Brighton SRA - Murray Lake

Total sites: 25, RV sites: 25, Central water, Vault/pit toilet, No showers, No RV dump, Tent & RV camping: $20, Weekends only, MI Recreation Passport required -non-residents: $9/day or $34/annual/residents: $12-$17/annual, Open May-Sep, Reservations accepted, Elev: 882ft/269m, Tel: 810-229-6566, Nearest town: Brighton. GPS: 42.508439, -83.816261

16 • D4 | Holly SRA - McGinnis Lake - Hickory

Total sites: 25, RV sites: 25, Elec sites: 25, Central water, Flush toilet, Free showers, RV dump, Tent & RV camping: $22-25, Also cabins, $20-$24 off-season, MI Recreation Passport required - non-residents: $9/day or $34/annual/residents: $12-$17/annual, Open Apr-Oct, Reservations accepted, Elev: 1031ft/314m, Tel: 248-634-8811, Nearest town: Holly. GPS: 42.822943, -83.530668

17 • D4 | Holly SRA - McGinnis Lake - Maple

Total sites: 40, RV sites: 40, Elec sites: 40, Central water, Flush toilet, Free showers, RV dump, Tent & RV camping: $22-34, Also cabins, $20-$24 off-season, MI Recreation Passport required - non-residents: $9/day or $34/annual/residents: $12-$17/annual, Open Mar-Nov, Reservations accepted, Elev: 1025ft/312m, Tel: 248-634-8811, Nearest town: Holly. GPS: 42.823962, -83.522196

18 • D4 | Holly SRA - McGinnis Lake - Oak

Total sites: 39, RV sites: 39, Elec sites: 39, Central water, Flush toilet, Free showers, RV dump, Tent & RV camping: $22-34, Also cabins, $20-$24 off-season, MI Recreation Passport required - non-residents: $9/day or $34/annual/residents: $12-$17/annual, Open Mar-Nov, Reservations accepted, Elev: 1046ft/319m, Tel: 248-634-8811, Nearest town: Holly. GPS: 42.824732, -83.525742

19 • D4 | Holly SRA - McGinnis Lake - Trillium

Total sites: 40, RV sites: 40, Elec sites: 40, Central water, Flush toilet, Free showers, RV dump, Tent & RV camping: $22-25, Also cabins, $20-$24 off-season, MI Recreation Passport required - non-residents: $9/day or $34/annual/residents: $12-$17/annual, Open Apr-Oct, Reservations accepted, Elev: 1033ft/315m, Tel: 248-634-8811, Nearest town: Holly. GPS: 42.825296, -83.529113

20 • D4 | Metamora-Hadley RA

Total sites: 214, RV sites: 214, Elec sites: 214, Central water, Flush toilet, Free showers, RV dump, Tent & RV camping: $22-30, Also cabins, $20 Nov-Mar, MI Recreation Passport required -non-residents: $9/day or $34/annual/residents: $12-$17/annual, Open Apr-Nov, Reservations accepted, Elev: 955ft/291m, Tel: 810-797-4439, Nearest town: Metamora. GPS: 42.942656, -83.350904

21 • D4 | Ortonville Rec Area - Equestrian

Total sites: 25, RV sites: 25, Central water, Vault/pit toilet, No showers, No RV dump, Tent & RV camping: $20, MI Recreation Passport required -non-residents: $9/day or $34/annual/residents: $12-$17/annual, Open Apr-Nov, Reservations accepted, Elev: 1073ft/327m, Tel: 810-797-4439, Nearest town: Ortonville. GPS: 42.896873, -83.409532

22 • D4 | Pinckney SRA - Bruin Lake

Total sites: 186, RV sites: 186, Elec sites: 186, Central water, Flush toilet, Free showers, RV dump, Tent & RV camping: $22-37, $20-$24 off-season, MI Recreation Passport required -non-residents: $9/day or $34/annual/residents: $12-$17/annual, Open Apr-Nov, Reservations accepted, Elev: 932ft/284m, Tel: 734-426-4913, Nearest town: Pinckney. GPS: 42.421886, -84.043718

23 • D4 | Pinckney SRA - Crooked Lake

Total sites: 25, RV sites: 25, Central water, Vault/pit toilet, No showers, No RV dump, Tent & RV camping: $20, MI Recreation Passport required -non-residents: $9/day or $34/annual/residents: $12-$17/annual, Open Apr-Nov, Reservations accepted, Elev: 942ft/287m, Tel: 734-426-4913, Nearest town: Pinckney. GPS: 42.421714, -83.980081

24 • D4 | Pontiac Lake RA - Equestrian

Total sites: 24, RV sites: 24, Central water, Vault/pit toilet, No showers, No RV dump, Tent & RV camping: $20, MI Recreation Passport required -non-residents: $9/day or $34/annual/residents: $12-$17/annual, Open Apr-Oct, Reservations accepted, Elev: 1053ft/321m, Tel: 248-666-1020, Nearest town: Waterford. GPS: 42.689121, -83.459049

25 • D4 | Pontiac Lake RA - Family

Total sites: 176, RV sites: 176, Elec sites: 176, Central water, Flush toilet, Free showers, RV dump, Tent & RV camping: $24-27, MI Recreation Passport required -non-residents: $9/day or $34/

annual/residents: $12-$17/annual, Open May-Oct, Reservations accepted, Elev: 1047ft/319m, Tel: 248-666-1020, Nearest town: Waterford. GPS: 42.686122, -83.471367

26 • D4 | Proud Lake SRA

Total sites: 130, RV sites: 130, Elec sites: 130, Central water, Flush toilet, Free showers, Tent & RV camping: $27-34, Also cabins, MI Recreation Passport required -non-residents: $9/day or $34/annual/residents: $12-$17/annual, Stay limit: 15 days, Open Apr-Nov, Reservations accepted, Elev: 919ft/280m, Tel: 248-685-2433, Nearest town: Commerce. GPS: 42.562832, -83.526181

27 • D4 | Waterloo SRA - Equestrian

Total sites: 25, RV sites: 25, Central water, Vault/pit toilet, No showers, No RV dump, Tent & RV camping: $20, MI Recreation Passport required -non-residents: $9/day or $34/annual/residents: $12-$17/annual, Open all year, Reservations not accepted, Elev: 979ft/298m, Tel: 734-475-8307, Nearest town: Chelsea. GPS: 42.334769, -84.129923

28 • D4 | Waterloo SRA - Green Lake

Total sites: 26, RV sites: 26, Central water, Vault/pit toilet, No showers, No RV dump, Tent & RV camping: $20, MI Recreation Passport required -non-residents: $9/day or $34/annual/residents: $12-$17/annual, Open Apr-Nov, Reservations not accepted, Elev: 942ft/287m, Tel: 734-475-8307, Nearest town: Chelsea. GPS: 42.365121, -84.071533

29 • D4 | Waterloo SRA - Sugarloaf

Total sites: 164, RV sites: 164, Elec sites: 164, Central water, Flush toilet, Free showers, RV dump, Tent & RV camping: $30-37, MI Recreation Passport required -non-residents: $9/day or $34/annual/residents: $12-$17/annual, Open May-Oct, Reservations accepted, Elev: 955ft/291m, Tel: 734-475-8307, Nearest town: Chelsea. GPS: 42.342510, -84.121510

30 • E3 | Lake Hudson Rec Area

Total sites: 50, RV sites: 50, Elec sites: 50, Central water, Vault/pit toilet, No showers, No RV dump, Tent & RV camping: $22-25, MI Recreation Passport required -non-residents: $9/day or $34/annual/residents: $12-$17/annual, Open Apr-Nov, Reservations accepted, Elev: 866ft/264m, Tel: 517-445-2265, Nearest town: Clayton. GPS: 41.825317, -84.259564

Minnesota

MANITOBA

ONTARIO

● 2

● 1

71

53

2

Bemidji

● 3

Lake Superior

59

2

371

Duluth

210

ND

94

MI

Fergus Falls

10

4

35

WISCONSIN

59

94

St. Cloud

12

10

SD

12

71

Minneapolis

212

St. Paul

MINNESOTA

35

14

71

90

90

90

Albert Lea

IOWA

Map	ID	Map	ID
B1	1	C2	4
B2	2-3		

Alphabetical List of Camping Areas

1 • B1 | Red River SRA - Sherlock Park

Total sites: 114, RV sites: 109, Elec sites: 98, Central water, Flush toilet, Free showers, No RV dump, Tents: $20/RVs: $32-40, Also walk-to sites, 98 Full hookups, $7 daily entrance fee, Generator hours: 0800-2200, Open May-Sep, Max Length: 60ft, Reservations accepted, Elev: 840ft/256m, Tel: 218-773-4950, Nearest town: East Grand Forks. GPS: 47.931801, -97.030524

2 • B2 | Big Bog SRA

Total sites: 31, RV sites: 31, Elec sites: 26, Central water, Flush toilet, Free showers, No RV dump, Tents: $23/RVs: $31, Also cabins, $7 daily entrance fee, Open all year, Max Length: 60ft, Elev: 1181ft/360m, Tel: 218-647-8592, Nearest town: Waskish. GPS: 48.173951, -94.511244

3 • B2 | La Salle Lake SRA

Total sites: 39, RV sites: 39, Elec sites: 39, Water at site, Flush toilet, Free showers, No RV dump, Tent & RV camping: $37, 39 Full hookups, Reservations accepted, Elev: 1503ft/458m, Tel: 218-699-7251, Nearest town: Solway. GPS: 47.343907, -95.161115

4 • C2 | Cuyuna Country SRA - Portsmouth CG

Total sites: 33, RV sites: 29, Elec sites: 18, Central water, Flush toilet, Free showers, No RV dump, Tents: $15/RVs: $23, $7 daily entrance fee, Open May-Oct, Reservations required, Elev: 1224ft/373m, Tel: 218-546-5926, Nearest town: Ironton. GPS: 46.491304, -93.972676

Mississippi

Map	ID	Map	ID
C3	1-3	D3	4-5

Alphabetical List of Camping Areas

1 • C3 | Dunns Falls - PHWD

Total sites: 15, RV sites: 15, No water, No toilets, Tent & RV camping: $15, Also cabins, 10% discount for military, Open all year, Reservations required, Elev: 315ft/96m, Tel: Info: 601-655-8550/Res: 800-748-9403, Nearest town: Enterprise. GPS: 32.228474, -88.821262

2 • C3 | Maynor Creek Waterpark - PHWD

Total sites: 69, RV sites: 69, Elec sites: 69, Water at site, Flush toilet, Free showers, RV dump, Tent & RV camping: $28-30, Also cabins, 10% discount for military, Open all year, Reservations required, Elev: 338ft/103m, Tel: 601-735-4365, Nearest town: Waynesboro. GPS: 31.654764, -88.721883

3 • C3 | Turkey Creek Water Park - PHWD

Total sites: 22, RV sites: 22, Elec sites: 22, Water at site, Flush toilet, Free showers, RV dump, Tent & RV camping: $28, Also cabins, 10% discount for military, Reservations required, Elev: 505ft/154m, Tel: 601-635-3314, Nearest town: Decatur. GPS: 32.407315, -89.153353

4 • D3 | Archusa Creek Waterpark - PHWD

Total sites: 69, RV sites: 44, Elec sites: 44, Central water, Flush toilet, Free showers, RV dump, Tents: $15/RVs: $25, Also cabins, 10% military discount, Generator hours: 0600-2200, Open all year, Reservations required, Elev: 282ft/86m, Tel: 601-776-6956, Nearest town: Quitman. GPS: 32.029828, -88.706908

5 • D3 | Okatibbee Lake Waterpark - PHWD

Total sites: 105, RV sites: 105, Elec sites: 105, Water at site, Flush toilet, Free showers, RV dump, Tents: $8/RVs: $28, Also cabins, 105 Full hookups, 10% discount for military, Open all year, Reservations required, Elev: 387ft/118m, Tel: 601-737-2370, Nearest town: Meridian. GPS: 32.497295, -88.781215

Missouri

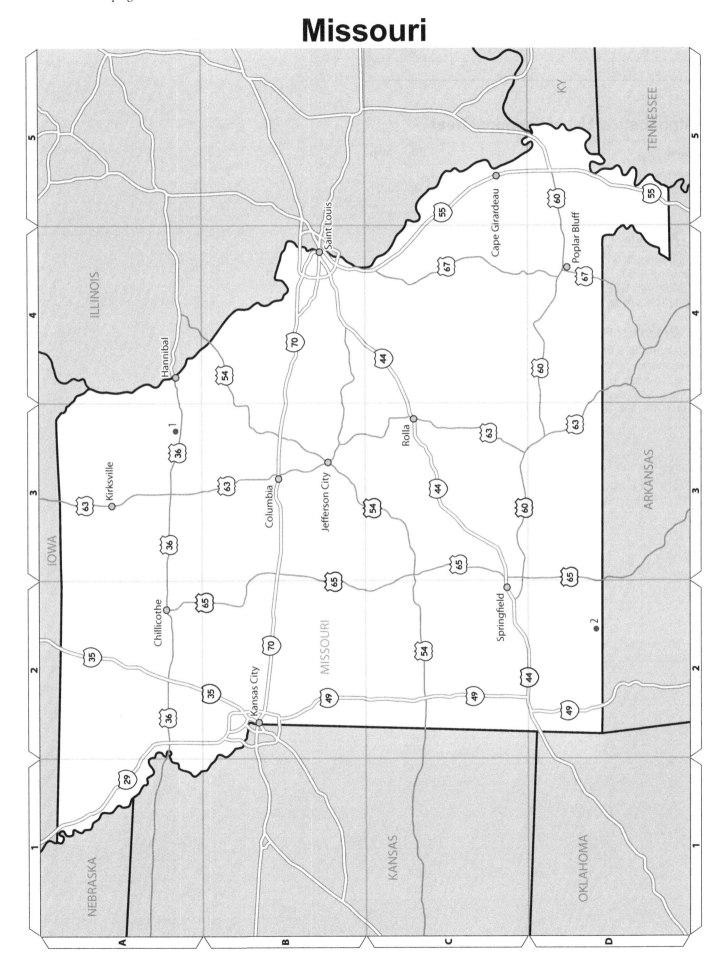

Map	ID	Map	ID
A3	1	D2	2

Alphabetical List of Camping Areas

Name	ID	Map
Hunnewell Lake RA - MDC	1	A3
Viney Creek Recreation Area	2	D2

1 • A3 | Hunnewell Lake RA - MDC

Total sites: 20, RV sites: 20, No water, Vault/pit toilet, Tent & RV camping: Free, Open all year, Reservations not accepted, Elev: 718ft/219m, Tel: 573-983-2201, Nearest town: Monroe City. GPS: 39.712105, -91.862734

2 • D2 | Viney Creek Recreation Area

Total sites: 46, RV sites: 46, Elec sites: 23, Water at site, Flush toilet, Free showers, RV dump, Tents: $16/RVs: $23-25, 1 family site - $40, No water 1 Nov-15 May - lower rates, Open all year, Max Length: 50ft, Reservations accepted, Elev: 928ft/283m, Tel: 417-334-4101, Nearest town: Golden. GPS: 36.564514, -93.675748

Nebraska

Map	ID	Map	ID
A2	1	C1	35
B1	2-6	C2	36-57
B2	7	C3	58-70
B3	8-20	C4	71-84
B4	21-26	C5	85-118
B5	27-34		

Alphabetical List of Camping Areas

1 • A2 | Cottonwood Lake SRA

Total sites: 30, RV sites: 30, Central water, Vault/pit toilet, No showers, No RV dump, Tent & RV camping: $15, $8 ($6 in-state residents) daily entrance fee, Stay limit: 14 days, Open all year, Reservations not accepted, Elev: 3235ft/986m, Tel: 308-684-3428, Nearest town: Merriman. GPS: 42.914595, -101.678919

2 • B1 | Box Butte SRA

Total sites: 54, RV sites: 54, Elec sites: 14, Water at site, Vault/pit toilet, No showers, No RV dump, Tents: $15/RVs: $25-30, $8 ($6 in-state residents) daily entrance fee, Stay limit: 14 days, Open all year, Reservations not accepted, Elev: 4042ft/1232m, Tel: 308-665-2903, Nearest town: Hemingford. GPS: 42.463836, -103.077676

3 • B1 | Bridgeport SRA

Total sites: 130, RV sites: 130, Central water, Vault/pit toilet, No showers, RV dump, Tent & RV camping: $15, $8 ($6 in-state residents) daily entrance fee, Stay limit: 14 days, Open all year, Reservations not accepted, Elev: 3688ft/1124m, Tel: 308-436-3777, Nearest town: Bridgeport. GPS: 41.677498, -103.114718

4 • B1 | Lake Minatare SRA - Butte View

Total sites: 49, RV sites: 49, Elec sites: 49, Central water, Vault/pit toilet, No showers, No RV dump, Tent & RV camping: $30, $8 ($6 in-state residents) daily entrance fee, Stay limit: 14 days, Open Jan-Oct, Reservations not accepted, Elev: 4131ft/1259m, Tel: 308-783-2911, Nearest town: Scottsbluff. GPS: 41.942635, -103.475972

5 • B1 | Lake Minatare SRA - Lake View Point

Total sites: 52, RV sites: 52, Elec sites: 52, Central water, Flush toilet, Free showers, RV dump, Tent & RV camping: $30, $8 ($6 in-state residents) daily entrance fee, Stay limit: 14 days, Open Jan-Oct, Reservations accepted, Elev: 4131ft/1259m, Tel: 308-783-2911, Nearest town: Scottsbluff. GPS: 41.931573, -103.502245

6 • B1 | Wildcat Hills SRA

Total sites: 5, RV sites: 5, Central water, Vault/pit toilet, No showers, No RV dump, Tent & RV camping: $15, $8 ($6 in-state residents) daily entrance fee, Stay limit: 14 days, Open all year, Reservations not accepted, Elev: 4636ft/1413m, Tel: 308-436-3777, Nearest town: Gering. GPS: 41.707041, -103.673963

7 • B2 | Walgren Lake SRA

Total sites: 40, RV sites: 40, Central water, Vault/pit toilet, No showers, No RV dump, Tent & RV camping: $10, $8 ($6 in-state residents) daily entrance fee, Stay limit: 14 days, Open all year, Reservations not accepted, Elev: 3753ft/1144m, Tel: 308-432-6167, Nearest town: Hay Springs. GPS: 42.640963, -102.628097

8 • B3 | Calamus Reservoir SRA - Hannamon Bayou

Dispersed sites, Central water, Flush toilet, Free showers, No RV dump, Tent & RV camping: $15, $8 ($6 in-state residents) daily entrance fee, Stay limit: 14 days, Open all year, Elev: 2247ft/685m, Tel: 308-346-5666, Nearest town: Burwell. GPS: 41.924711, -99.338347

9 • B3 | Calamus Reservoir SRA - Homestead Knolls

Total sites: 83, RV sites: 83, Elec sites: 83, Water at site, Flush toilet, Free showers, No RV dump, Tent & RV camping: $30, $8 ($6 in-state residents) daily entrance fee, Stay limit: 14 days, Open all year, Max Length: 20ft, Reservations accepted, Elev: 2290ft/698m, Tel: 308-346-5666, Nearest town: Burwell. GPS: 41.848551, -99.217162

10 • B3 | Calamus Reservoir SRA - Nunda Shoal

Total sites: 39, RV sites: 39, Elec sites: 39, Central water, Flush toilet, Free showers, RV dump, Tent & RV camping: $30, $8 ($6 in-state residents) daily entrance fee, Stay limit: 14 days, Open all year, Reservations accepted, Elev: 2251ft/686m, Tel: 308-346-5666, Nearest town: Burwell. GPS: 41.867036, -99.272445

11 • B3 | Calamus Reservoir SRA - Valley View Flat

Total sites: 12, RV sites: 10, Elec sites: 10, Central water, Flush toilet, Free showers, Tents: $15/RVs: $30, $8 ($6 in-state residents) daily entrance fee, Stay limit: 14 days, Open all year, Elev: 2264ft/690m, Tel: 308-346-5666, Nearest town: Burwell. GPS: 41.907164, -99.298857

12 • B3 | Cub Creek Rec Area (Northern) - MNNRD

Dispersed sites, Central water, Vault/pit toilet, Tent & RV camping: Free, Open all year, Reservations not accepted, Elev: 2405ft/733m, Tel: 402-376-3241, Nearest town: Springview. GPS: 42.824523, -99.912506

13 • B3 | Keller Park SRA

Total sites: 50, RV sites: 40, Elec sites: 25, Central water, Flush toilet, No showers, RV dump, Tents: $10-15/RVs: $25, $8 ($6 in-state residents) daily entrance fee, Stay limit: 14 days, Open all year, Reservations not accepted, Elev: 2165ft/660m, Tel: 402-684-2921, Nearest town: Ainsworth. GPS: 42.668189, -99.775236

14 • B3 | Long Lake SRA

Total sites: 10, RV sites: 10, Central water, Vault/pit toilet, No showers, No RV dump, Tents: $10-15/RVs: $15, $8 ($6 in-state residents) daily entrance fee, Stay limit: 14 days, Open all year, Reservations not accepted, Elev: 2723ft/830m, Tel: 402-684-2921, Nearest town: Johnstown. GPS: 42.283733, -100.094111

15 • B3 | Merritt Reservoir SRA - Beeds Landing

Total sites: 20, RV sites: 10, Elec sites: 10, Central water, Vault/pit toilet, RV dump, Tents: $15/RVs: $30, $8 ($6 in-state residents) daily entrance fee, Stay limit: 14 days, Open all year, Reservations accepted, Elev: 2966ft/904m, Tel: 402-389-0672, Nearest town: Valentine. GPS: 42.591819, -100.890386

16 • B3 | Merritt Reservoir SRA - Boardman

Total sites: 10, RV sites: 10, Elec sites: 10, Central water, Vault/pit toilet, Tent & RV camping: $30, $8 ($6 in-state residents) daily entrance fee, Stay limit: 14 days, Reservations accepted, Elev: 2957ft/901m, Tel: 402-389-0672, Nearest town: Valentine. GPS: 42.581447, -100.890655

17 • B3 | Merritt Reservoir SRA - Cedar Bay

Total sites: 47, RV sites: 39, Elec sites: 39, Water at site, Flush toilet, Free showers, RV dump, Tents: $15/RVs: $25-30, $8 ($6 in-state residents) daily entrance fee, Stay limit: 14 days, Open all year, Reservations accepted, Elev: 2963ft/903m, Tel: 402-389-0672, Nearest town: Valentine. GPS: 42.598074, -100.896242

18 • B3 | Merritt Reservoir SRA - West Beeds

Total sites: 11, RV sites: 10, Elec sites: 10, Central water, Vault/pit toilet, Tents: $15/RVs: $30, $8 ($6 in-state residents) daily entrance fee, Stay limit: 14 days, Open all year, Reservations accepted, Elev: 2959ft/902m, Tel: 402-389-0672, Nearest town: Valentine. GPS: 42.592982, -100.892881

19 • B3 | Merritt Reservoir SRA - Willow Cove

Total sites: 21, RV sites: 21, Elec sites: 21, Central water, Vault/pit toilet, RV dump, Tent & RV camping: $30, $8 ($6 in-state residents) daily entrance fee, Stay limit: 14 days, Open all year, Reservations not accepted, Elev: 2959ft/902m, Tel: 402-389-0672, Nearest town: Valentine. GPS: 42.622188, -100.862395

20 • B3 | Victoria Springs SRA

Total sites: 81, RV sites: 81, Elec sites: 21, Central water, Flush toilet, Free showers, RV dump, Tents: $15/RVs: $25-30, Also cabins, $8 ($6 in-state residents) daily entrance fee, Stay limit: 14 days, Open May-Nov, Reservations accepted, Elev: 2543ft/775m, Tel: 308-749-2235, Nearest town: Anselmo. GPS: 41.610166, -99.750159

21 • B4 | Lewis and Clark SRA - Bloomfield

Total sites: 20, RV sites: 12, Elec sites: 12, Central water, Flush toilet, Free showers, No RV dump, Tent & RV camping: $15, $8 ($6 in-state residents) daily entrance fee, Stay limit: 14 days, Open all year, Elev: 1214ft/370m, Tel: 402-388-4169, Nearest town: Crofton. GPS: 42.840071, -97.637558

22 • B4 | Lewis and Clark SRA - Burbach

Total sites: 97, RV sites: 97, Elec sites: 73, Central water, Flush toilet, Free showers, No RV dump, Tents: $15/RVs: $25-30, Also cabins, $8 ($6 in-state residents) daily entrance fee, Stay limit: 14 days, Open all year, Reservations accepted, Elev: 1217ft/371m, Tel: 402-388-4169, Nearest town: Crofton. GPS: 42.837212, -97.592405

23 • B4 | Lewis and Clark SRA - Weigand

Total sites: 103, RV sites: 95, Elec sites: 95, Central water, Flush toilet, Free showers, No RV dump, Tents: $15/RVs: $25-30, $8 ($6 in-state residents) daily entrance fee, Stay limit: 14 days, Open all year, Reservations accepted, Elev: 1207ft/368m, Tel: 402-388-4169, Nearest town: Crofton. GPS: 42.836084, -97.572266

24 • B4 | Maple Creek Rec Area - LENRD

Total sites: 60, RV sites: 50, Elec sites: 50, Water available, Flush toilet, Free showers, RV dump, Tents: $8/RVs: $20, Overflow camping $8, Elev: 1660ft/506m, Tel: 402-371-7313, Nearest town: Leigh. GPS: 41.712010, -97.245186

25 • B4 | Willow Creek SRA - Equestrian

Total sites: 15, RV sites: 15, Elec sites: 10, Water at site, Vault/pit toilet, Tents: $20/RVs: $35, $8 ($6 in-state residents) daily entrance fee, Stay limit: 14 days, Open all year, Reservations accepted, Elev: 1634ft/498m, Tel: 402-329-4053, Nearest town: Pierce. GPS: 42.172952, -97.560975

26 • B4 | Willow Creek SRA - Willow Way

Total sites: 101, RV sites: 101, Elec sites: 101, Water at site, Flush toilet, Free showers, RV dump, Tent & RV camping: $25-30, $8 ($6 in-state residents) daily entrance fee, Stay limit: 14 days, Open all year, Reservations not accepted, Elev: 1634ft/498m, Tel: 402-329-4053, Nearest town: Pierce. GPS: 42.174102, -97.568378

27 • B5 | Danish Alps SRA - Jones Creek

Total sites: 66, RV sites: 44, Elec sites: 44, Water at site, Flush toilet, No showers, No RV dump, Tents: $15/RVs: $25-30, $8 ($6 in-state residents) daily entrance fee, Stay limit: 14 days, Open all year, Reservations not accepted, Elev: 1237ft/377m, Tel: 402-632-4106, Nearest town: Hubbard. GPS: 42.382717, -96.581447

28 • B5 | Danish Alps SRA - Pigeon Creek Equestrian

Total sites: 29, RV sites: 29, Elec sites: 29, Water at site, Flush toilet, No showers, No RV dump, Tent & RV camping: $35, $8 ($6 in-state residents) daily entrance fee, Stay limit: 14 days, Open all year, Reservations not accepted, Elev: 1209ft/369m, Tel: 402-632-4106, Nearest town: Hubbard. GPS: 42.375323, -96.582534

29 • B5 | Dead Timber SRA

Total sites: 21, RV sites: 17, Elec sites: 17, Central water, Vault/pit toilet, No showers, No RV dump, Tents: $10/RVs: $25, $8 ($6 in-state residents) daily entrance fee, Stay limit: 14 days, Open all year, Reservations not accepted, Elev: 1306ft/398m, Tel: 402-727-2922, Nearest town: Scribner. GPS: 41.719928, -96.685073

30 • B5 | Fremont Lakes SRA - Area 2

Total sites: 11, RV sites: 11, Elec sites: 11, Central water, Flush toilet, Free showers, No RV dump, Tent & RV camping: $25, $8 ($6 in-state residents) daily entrance fee, Stay limit: 14 days, Open all year, Reservations accepted, Elev: 1214ft/370m, Tel: 402-727-2922, Nearest town: Fremont. GPS: 41.450825, -96.567079

31 • B5 | Fremont Lakes SRA - Pathfinder

Total sites: 97, RV sites: 97, Elec sites: 97, Central water, Flush toilet, Free showers, RV dump, Tents: $25/RVs: $25-30, 600 dispersed sites, $8 ($6 in-state residents) daily entrance fee, Stay limit: 14 days, Open all year, Max Length: 80ft, Reservations accepted, Elev: 1217ft/371m, Tel: 402-727-2922, Nearest town: Fremont. GPS: 41.443079, -96.554132

32 • B5 | Fremont Lakes SRA - Victory Lake

Total sites: 85, RV sites: 71, Elec sites: 71, Water at site, Flush toilet, Free showers, RV dump, Tents: $15/RVs: $25-30, 600 dispersed sites, $8 ($6 in-state residents) daily entrance fee, Stay limit: 14 days, Open all year, Max Length: 60ft, Reservations accepted,

Elev: 1220ft/372m, Tel: 402-727-2922, Nearest town: Fremont. GPS: 41.440070, -96.545180

33 • B5 | Pelican Point SRA

Total sites: 6, RV sites: 6, Central water, Vault/pit toilet, No showers, No RV dump, Tent & RV camping: $15, $8 ($6 in-state residents) daily entrance fee, Stay limit: 14 days, Open all year, Reservations not accepted, Elev: 1024ft/312m, Tel: 402-468-5611, Nearest town: Tekamah. GPS: 41.834047, -96.112786

34 • B5 | Summit Lake SRA

Total sites: 67, RV sites: 45, Elec sites: 30, Water at site, Vault/pit toilet, No showers, RV dump, Tents: $15/RVs: $25-30, $8 ($6 in-state residents) daily entrance fee, Stay limit: 14 days, Open all year, Reservations not accepted, Elev: 1148ft/350m, Tel: 402-374-1727, Nearest town: Tekamah. GPS: 41.762186, -96.299698

35 • C1 | Oliver Reservoir SRA

Total sites: 175, RV sites: 50, Central water, Vault/pit toilet, No showers, No RV dump, Tent & RV camping: Donation, Stay limit: 14 days, Open all year, Elev: 4833ft/1473m, Tel: 308-254-2377, Nearest town: Kimball. GPS: 41.231185, -103.830738

36 • C2 | Champion Lake SRA

Total sites: 6, RV sites: 6, Elec sites: 6, Central water, Vault/pit toilet, No showers, No RV dump, Tents: $7/RVs: $12, Stay limit: 14 days, Open all year, Elev: 3261ft/994m, Tel: 402-471-1623, Nearest town: Champion. GPS: 40.472415, -101.751697

37 • C2 | Enders Reservoir SRA - Center Dam

Total sites: 8, RV sites: 8, Elec sites: 8, Central water, Flush toilet, Pay showers, RV dump, Tent & RV camping: $30, $8 ($6 in-state residents) daily entrance fee, Also 200 dispersed sites around lake, Stay limit: 14 days, Open all year, Reservations not accepted, Elev: 3140ft/957m, Tel: 402-471-1623, Nearest town: Imperial. GPS: 40.437395, -101.523175

38 • C2 | Enders Reservoir SRA - Main

Total sites: 24, RV sites: 24, Elec sites: 24, Central water, Flush toilet, Pay showers, RV dump, Tent & RV camping: $30, $8 ($6 in-state residents) daily entrance fee, Also 200 dispersed sites around lake, Stay limit: 14 days, Open all year, Reservations not accepted, Elev: 3149ft/960m, Tel: 402-471-1623, Nearest town: Imperial. GPS: 40.432628, -101.520191

39 • C2 | Lake McConaughy SRA - Arthur Bay CG

Dispersed sites, Central water, Flush toilet, Pay showers, RV dump, Tent & RV camping: $15-20, Sep-May: $10, $8 ($6 in-state residents) daily entrance fee, Stay limit: 14 days, Open all year, Reservations required, Elev: 3274ft/998m, Tel: 308-284-8800, Nearest town: Ogallala. GPS: 41.251383, -101.725428

40 • C2 | Lake McConaughy SRA - Cedar View

Total sites: 102, RV sites: 102, Elec sites: 85, Water at site, Flush toilet, Pay showers, RV dump, Tents: $15-20/RVs: $30-35, $8 ($6 in-state residents) daily entrance fee, Sep-May: $10/$25, Stay limit: 14 days, Open all year, Reservations required, Elev: 3278ft/999m, Tel: 308-284-8800, Nearest town: Ogallala. GPS: 41.292491, -101.935165

41 • C2 | Lake McConaughy SRA - Eagle Canyon

Total sites: 100, RV sites: 100, Central water, Vault/pit toilet, No showers, No RV dump, Tent & RV camping: $20-25, $8 ($6 in-state residents) daily entrance fee, Sep-May: $15, Stay limit: 14 days, Open all year, Reservations required, Elev: 3262ft/994m, Tel: 308-284-8800, Nearest town: Ogallala. GPS: 41.269841, -101.954989

42 • C2 | Lake McConaughy SRA - Lakeview

Total sites: 30, RV sites: 30, Central water, Flush toilet, Free showers, No RV dump, Tent & RV camping: $20-25, $8 ($6 in-state residents) daily entrance fee, Sep-May: $15, Stay limit: 14 days, Open all year, Reservations required, Elev: 3273ft/998m, Tel: 308-284-8800, Nearest town: Ogallala. GPS: 41.236125, -101.843183

43 • C2 | Lake McConaughy SRA - Lemoyne

Total sites: 200, RV sites: 200, Central water, Vault/pit toilet, No showers, No RV dump, Tent & RV camping: $20-25, $8 ($6 in-state residents) daily entrance fee, Sep-May: $15, Stay limit: 14 days, Open all year, Reservations required, Elev: 3297ft/1005m, Tel: 308-284-8800, Nearest town: Ogallala. GPS: 41.271136, -101.816103

44 • C2 | Lake McConaughy SRA - Little Thunder CG

Total sites: 42, RV sites: 42, Elec sites: 42, Water at site, Flush toilet, Pay showers, No RV dump, Tent & RV camping: $30-40, 8 Full hookups, No water in winter, Sep-May: $25-$30, $8 ($6 in-state residents) daily entrance fee, Stay limit: 14 days, Open all year, Reservations required, Elev: 3274ft/998m, Tel: 308-284-8800, Nearest town: Ogallala. GPS: 41.251098, -101.711799

45 • C2 | Lake McConaughy SRA - Lone Eagle CG

Total sites: 84, RV sites: 84, Elec sites: 84, Water at site, Flush toilet, Pay showers, RV dump, Tent & RV camping: $35-40, 84 Full hookups, No water in winter, Sep-May: $30, $8 ($6 in-state residents) daily entrance fee, Stay limit: 14 days, Open all year, Reservations required, Elev: 3291ft/1003m, Tel: 308-284-8800, Nearest town: Ogallala. GPS: 41.255235, -101.757937

46 • C2 | Lake McConaughy SRA - Martin Bay CG

Total sites: 40, RV sites: 20, Central water, Flush toilet, No showers, RV dump, Tent & RV camping: $15-20, May-Sep: $10, $8 ($6 in-state residents) daily entrance fee, Stay limit: 14 days, Open all year, Reservations required, Elev: 3307ft/1008m, Tel: 308-284-8800, Nearest town: Ogallala. GPS: 41.252957, -101.689373

47 • C2 | Lake McConaughy SRA - No Name Bay

Dispersed sites, Central water, Flush toilet, Free showers, No RV dump, Tent & RV camping: $20-25, $8 ($6 in-state residents) daily entrance fee, Sep-May: $15, Stay limit: 14 days, Open all year, Reservations required, Elev: 3320ft/1012m, Tel: 308-284-8800, Nearest town: Ogallala. GPS: 41.253909, -101.705694

48 • C2 | Lake McConaughy SRA - Sandy Beach

Dispersed sites, Central water, Flush toilet, Free showers, RV dump, Tent & RV camping: $20-25, $8 ($6 in-state residents) daily entrance fee, Sep-May: $15, Stay limit: 14 days, Reservations required, Elev: 3278ft/999m, Tel: 308-284-8800, Nearest town: Ogallala. GPS: 41.258078, -101.768557

49 • C2 | Lake McConaughy SRA - Theis Bay

Dispersed sites, Central water, Flush toilet, Free showers, RV dump, Tent & RV camping: $15, $8 ($6 in-state residents) daily entrance fee, Sep-May: $15, Stay limit: 14 days, Reservations required, Elev: 3285ft/1001m, Tel: 308-284-8800, Nearest town: Ogallala. GPS: 41.252263, -101.742744

50 • C2 | Lake Ogallala SRA - East

Total sites: 82, RV sites: 82, Elec sites: 82, Water at site, Flush toilet, Free showers, No RV dump, Tent & RV camping: $30, $8 ($6 in-state residents) daily entrance fee, Stay limit: 14 days, Open all year, Reservations accepted, Elev: 3143ft/958m, Tel: 308-284-8800, Nearest town: Ogallala. GPS: 41.226033, -101.662318

51 • C2 | Lake Ogallala SRA - West

Dispersed sites, Central water, Vault/pit toilet, No showers, No RV dump, Tent & RV camping: $15, $8 ($6 in-state residents) daily entrance fee, Stay limit: 14 days, Open all year, Reservations accepted, Elev: 3128ft/953m, Tel: 308-284-8800, Nearest town: Ogallala. GPS: 41.222028, -101.667038

52 • C2 | Rock Creek Lake SRA

Total sites: 43, RV sites: 43, Central water, Vault/pit toilet, No showers, No RV dump, Tent & RV camping: $15, $8 ($6 in-state residents) daily entrance fee, Stay limit: 14 days, Reservations not accepted, Elev: 3218ft/981m, Tel: 308-737-6577, Nearest town: Parks . GPS: 40.088436, -101.762288

53 • C2 | Sutherland Reservoir SRA - Inlet Area

Total sites: 25, RV sites: 25, Central water, Vault/pit toilet, No showers, No RV dump, Tent & RV camping: $10-15, $8 ($6 in-state residents) daily entrance fee, Stay limit: 14 days, Open all year, Reservations not accepted, Elev: 3077ft/938m, Tel: 308-535-8025, Nearest town: Sutherland. GPS: 41.091908, -101.156944

54 • C2 | Sutherland Reservoir SRA - Outlet Area

Total sites: 25, RV sites: 25, Central water, Vault/pit toilet, No showers, No RV dump, Tent & RV camping: $10-15, $8 ($6 in-state residents) daily entrance fee, Stay limit: 14 days, Open all year, Reservations not accepted, Elev: 3041ft/927m, Tel: 308-535-8025, Nearest town: Sutherland. GPS: 41.103318, -101.102885

55 • C2 | Sutherland Reservoir SRA - Westshore Area

Total sites: 25, RV sites: 25, Central water, Vault/pit toilet, No showers, No RV dump, Tent & RV camping: $10-15, $8 ($6 in-state residents) daily entrance fee, Stay limit: 14 days, Open all year, Reservations not accepted, Elev: 3074ft/937m, Tel: 308-535-8025, Nearest town: Sutherland. GPS: 41.104607, -101.159873

56 • C2 | Swanson Reservoir SRA - Macklin Bay

Total sites: 17, RV sites: 17, Elec sites: 17, Central water, Flush toilet, Free showers, RV dump, Tent & RV camping: $30, $8 ($6 in-state residents) daily entrance fee, Stay limit: 14 days, Open all year, Reservations not accepted, Elev: 2822ft/860m, Tel: 402-471-1623, Nearest town: Trenton. GPS: 40.174005, -101.099036

57 • C2 | Swanson Reservoir SRA - Spring Canyon

Total sites: 47, RV sites: 47, Elec sites: 47, Central water, Flush toilet, Free showers, RV dump, Tent & RV camping: $25-30, $8 ($6 in-state residents) daily entrance fee, Stay limit: 14 days, Open all year, Reservations not accepted, Elev: 2763ft/842m, Tel: 402-471-1623, Nearest town: Trenton. GPS: 40.145363, -101.072371

58 • C3 | Buffalo Bill Ranch SRA

Total sites: 31, RV sites: 31, Elec sites: 23, Water at site, Vault/pit toilet, No showers, No RV dump, Tents: $15/RVs: $25-30, $8 ($6 in-state residents) daily entrance fee, Stay limit: 14 days, Open all year, Reservations not accepted, Elev: 2816ft/858m, Tel: 308-535-8035, Nearest town: North Platte. GPS: 41.171919, -100.789169

59 • C3 | Fort Kearny SRA - East CG

Total sites: 10, RV sites: 10, Elec sites: 10, Central water, Vault/pit toilet, No showers, RV dump, Tent & RV camping: $30, $8 ($6 in-state residents) daily entrance fee, Stay limit: 14 days, Open all year, Reservations not accepted, Elev: 2112ft/644m, Tel: 308-865-5305, Nearest town: Kearny. GPS: 40.653726, -98.985648

60 • C3 | Fort Kearny SRA - West CG

Total sites: 110, RV sites: 110, Elec sites: 94, Water at site, Flush toilet, Free showers, RV dump, Tents: $15/RVs: $25-30, $8 ($6 in-state residents) daily entrance fee, Stay limit: 14 days, Open all year, Reservations accepted, Elev: 2123ft/647m, Tel: 308-865-5305, Nearest town: Kearny. GPS: 40.653445, -98.996849

61 • C3 | Gallagher Canyon SRA

Total sites: 24, RV sites: 24, No water, Vault/pit toilet, No showers, No RV dump, Tent & RV camping: $10, $8 ($6 in-state residents) daily entrance fee, Stay limit: 14 days, Open all year, Elev: 2667ft/813m, Tel: 308-785-2685, Nearest town: Cozad. GPS: 40.734273, -99.979238

62 • C3 | Johnson Lake SRA - Main

Total sites: 82, RV sites: 82, Elec sites: 82, Water at site, Flush toilet, Free showers, RV dump, Tent & RV camping: $25-30, $8 ($6 in-state residents) daily entrance fee, Stay limit: 14 days, Open all year, Max Length: 42ft, Reservations accepted, Elev: 2644ft/806m, Tel: 308-785-2685, Nearest town: Lexington. GPS: 40.684326, -99.828125

63 • C3 | Johnson Lake SRA - South Inlet

Total sites: 30, RV sites: 30, Elec sites: 30, Water at site, Flush toilet, Free showers, RV dump, Tent & RV camping: $25-30, $8 ($6 in-state residents) daily entrance fee, Stay limit: 14 days, Open all year, Max Length: 42ft, Reservations accepted, Elev: 2628ft/801m, Tel: 308-785-2685, Nearest town: Lexington. GPS: 40.695591, -99.871369

64 • C3 | Lake Maloney SRA

Total sites: 256, RV sites: 56, Elec sites: 56, Water at site, Flush toilet, Pay showers, RV dump, Tents: $10/RVs: $30, 200 dispersed sites, $8 ($6 in-state residents) daily entrance fee, Stay limit: 14 days, Reservations not accepted, Elev: 3012ft/918m, Tel: 308-535-8025, Nearest town: North Platte. GPS: 41.047758, -100.796176

65 • C3 | Medicine Creek SRA - Shady Bay

Total sites: 76, RV sites: 76, Elec sites: 76, Central water, Flush toilet, Free showers, RV dump, Tent & RV camping: $25-30, $8 ($6 in-state residents) daily entrance fee, Stay limit: 14 days, Open Apr-Dec, Reservations accepted, Elev: 2408ft/734m, Tel: 308-697-4667, Nearest town: Cambridge. GPS: 40.386795, -100.221214

66 • C3 | Medicine Creek SRA - Trail 12

Total sites: 18, RV sites: 18, Central water, Vault/pit toilet, No showers, No RV dump, Tent & RV camping: $15, $8 ($6 in-state residents) daily entrance fee, Stay limit: 14 days, Open Apr-Dec, Reservations accepted, Elev: 2408ft/734m, Tel: 308-697-4667, Nearest town: Cambridge. GPS: 40.417177, -100.224063

67 • C3 | Medicine Creek SRA - U Bay

Total sites: 8, RV sites: 8, Central water, Vault/pit toilet, No showers, No RV dump, Tent & RV camping: $15, $8 ($6 in-state residents) daily entrance fee, Stay limit: 14 days, Open Apr-Dec, Reservations accepted, Elev: 2428ft/740m, Tel: 308-697-4667, Nearest town: Cambridge. GPS: 40.382138, -100.230752

68 • C3 | Red Willow Reservoir SRA - Willow View

Total sites: 48, RV sites: 48, Elec sites: 48, Water at site, Vault/pit toilet, No showers, RV dump, Tent & RV camping: $25-30, $8 ($6 in-state residents) daily entrance fee, Stay limit: 14 days, Open all year, Reservations not accepted, Elev: 2651ft/808m, Tel: 402-471-1623, Nearest town: McCook. GPS: 40.364565, -100.662365

69 • C3 | Sandy Channel SRA

Total sites: 30, RV sites: 30, Central water, Vault/pit toilet, Tent & RV camping: $10-15, $8 ($6 in-state residents) daily entrance fee, Stay limit: 14 days, Reservations not accepted, Elev: 2267ft/691m, Tel: 308-865-5305, Nearest town: Elm Creek. GPS: 40.668641, -99.377604

70 • C3 | Union Pacific SRA

Total sites: 5, RV sites: 5, Central water, Flush toilet, No showers, No RV dump, Tent & RV camping: $10, $8 ($6 in-state residents) daily entrance fee, Stay limit: 14 days, Open all year, Reservations not accepted, Elev: 2218ft/676m, Tel: 308-865-5305, Nearest town: Kearney. GPS: 40.678898, -99.252975

71 • C4 | Alexandria SRA

Total sites: 53, RV sites: 53, Elec sites: 45, Central water, No toilets, No showers, RV dump, Tents: $15/RVs: $25-30, $8 ($6 in-state residents) daily entrance fee, Stay limit: 14 days, Open all year, Reservations not accepted, Elev: 1421ft/433m, Tel: 402-729-5777, Nearest town: Alexandria. GPS: 40.232695, -97.336628

72 • C4 | Bruce I. Anderson RA - NNRD

Total sites: 18, RV sites: 12, Elec sites: 12, Water available, Flush toilet, No showers, RV dump, Tents: $5/RVs: $15, Open all year, Elev: 1640ft/500m, Tel: 402-362-6601, Nearest town: York. GPS: 40.869782, -97.626143

73 • C4 | Davis Creek Rec Area - LLNRD

Total sites: 67, RV sites: 42, Elec sites: 42, Central water, Flush toilet, Tent & RV camping: Free, Open all year, Reservations not accepted, Elev: 2111ft/643m, Nearest town: North Loup. GPS: 41.419311, -98.765885

74 • C4 | DLD SRA

Dispersed sites, No water, No toilets, Tent & RV camping: $10, No fee station- can pay at Mormon Island SRA, Stay limit: 14 days, Open all year, Elev: 1900ft/579m, Tel: 308-385-6211, Nearest town: Hastings. GPS: 40.581890, -98.289790

75 • C4 | Mormon Island SRA - Cedar

Total sites: 36, RV sites: 36, Elec sites: 35, Water at site, Flush toilet, Free showers, RV dump, Tents: $15/RVs: $25-30, $8 ($6 in-state residents) daily entrance fee, Stay limit: 14 days, Open all year, Reservations accepted, Elev: 1877ft/572m, Tel: 308-385-6211, Nearest town: Grand Island. GPS: 40.825138, -98.366604

76 • C4 | Mormon Island SRA - Cottonwood

Total sites: 34, RV sites: 34, Elec sites: 34, Central water, Flush toilet, Free showers, RV dump, Tent & RV camping: $25-30, $8 ($6 in-state residents) daily entrance fee, Stay limit: 14 days, Open all year, Max Length: 78ft, Reservations accepted, Elev: 1877ft/572m, Tel: 308-385-6211, Nearest town: Grand Island. GPS: 40.826097, -98.370322

77 • C4 | North Loup SRA

Total sites: 10, RV sites: 10, Central water, Vault/pit toilet, No showers, No RV dump, Tent & RV camping: $10, $8 ($6 in-state residents) daily entrance fee, Stay limit: 14 days, Open all year, Reservations not accepted, Elev: 1772ft/540m, Tel: 308-385-6211, Nearest town: St. Paul. GPS: 41.263958, -98.453804

78 • C4 | Pioneer Trails RA - NNRD

Total sites: 10, RV sites: 10, Elec sites: 10, Water available, Vault/pit toilet, Tent & RV camping: Fee unk, Open all year, Reservations not accepted, Elev: 1785ft/544m, Tel: 402-362-6601, Nearest town: Aurora. GPS: 40.882777, -97.969841

79 • C4 | Rock Creek Station SRA - Family

Total sites: 35, RV sites: 25, Elec sites: 25, Central water, Flush toilet, Free showers, RV dump, Tents: $15/RVs: $25, $8 ($6 in-state residents) daily entrance fee, Stay limit: 14 days, Open all year, Reservations accepted, Elev: 1371ft/418m, Tel: 402-729-5777, Nearest town: Fairbury. GPS: 40.111227, -97.065285

80 • C4 | Rock Creek Station SRA - Horse Camp

Total sites: 10, RV sites: 10, Central water, Vault/pit toilet, No showers, No RV dump, Tent & RV camping: $20, $8 ($6 in-state residents) daily entrance fee, Stay limit: 14 days, Open all year, Reservations not accepted, Elev: 1378ft/420m, Tel: 402-729-5777, Nearest town: Fairbury. GPS: 40.113395, -97.064787

81 • C4 | Sherman Reservoir SRA

Total sites: 360, RV sites: 360, Central water, Flush toilet, Pay showers, RV dump, Tent & RV camping: $10-15, $8 ($6 in-state residents) daily entrance fee, Stay limit: 14 days, Open all year, Reservations not accepted, Elev: 2211ft/674m, Tel: 308-745-0230, Nearest town: Loup City. GPS: 41.287647, -98.899711

82 • C4 | Timber Point Rec Area - LPSNRD

Total sites: 3, RV sites: 3, No water, Vault/pit toilet, Tent & RV camping: Free, Open all year, Elev: 1503ft/458m, Tel: 402-476-2729, Nearest town: Brainard. GPS: 41.162184, -96.965988

83 • C4 | War Axe SRA

Total sites: 8, RV sites: 8, Central water, Vault/pit toilet, No showers, No RV dump, Tent & RV camping: $10, $8 ($6 in-state residents) daily entrance fee, Stay limit: 14 days, Open all year, Reservations not accepted, Elev: 2021ft/616m, Tel: 308-468-5700, Nearest town: Shelton. GPS: 40.724496, -98.735196

84 • C4 | Windmill SRA

Total sites: 89, RV sites: 89, Elec sites: 69, Water at site, Flush toilet, Free showers, RV dump, Tents: $15/RVs: $25-30, $8 ($6 in-state residents) daily entrance fee, Stay limit: 14 days, Open all year, Reservations accepted, Elev: 2057ft/627m, Tel: 308-468-5700, Nearest town: Gibbon. GPS: 40.708106, -98.838348

85 • C5 | Bluestem SRA

Total sites: 219, RV sites: 219, Central water, No toilets, No showers, RV dump, Tent & RV camping: $15, $8 ($6 in-state residents) daily entrance fee, Stay limit: 14 days, Open all year, Reservations not accepted, Elev: 1309ft/399m, Tel: 402-796-2362, Nearest town: Sprague. GPS: 40.631104, -96.797363

86 • C5 | Branched Oak SRA - Area 1 South Shore

Total sites: 128, RV sites: 120, Elec sites: 120, Water at site, Flush toilet, Free showers, RV dump, Tents: $15/RVs: $15-35, 12 Full hookups, $8 ($6 in-state residents) daily entrance fee, Stay limit: 14 days, Open all year, Reservations accepted, Elev: 1293ft/394m, Tel: 402-783-3400, Nearest town: Raymond. GPS: 40.958585, -96.872431

87 • C5 | Branched Oak SRA - Area 10

Total sites: 5, RV sites: 5, Central water, Vault/pit toilet, No showers, No RV dump, Tent & RV camping: $15, $8 ($6 in-state residents) daily entrance fee, Stay limit: 14 days, Open all year, Elev: 1316ft/401m, Tel: 402-783-3400, Nearest town: Raymond. GPS: 40.985778, -96.868226

88 • C5 | Branched Oak SRA - Area 11

Total sites: 12, RV sites: 12, Central water, Flush toilet, Pay showers, RV dump, Tent & RV camping: $10, $8 ($6 in-state residents) daily entrance fee, Stay limit: 14 days, Open all year, Elev: 1306ft/398m, Tel: 402-783-3400, Nearest town: Raymond. GPS: 40.980896, -96.857867

89 • C5 | Branched Oak SRA - Area 12

Total sites: 3, RV sites: 3, Central water, Vault/pit toilet, No showers, No RV dump, Tent & RV camping: $10, $8 ($6 in-state residents) daily entrance fee, Stay limit: 14 days, Open all year, Elev: 1299ft/396m, Tel: 402-783-3400, Nearest town: Raymond. GPS: 40.982218, -96.850507

90 • C5 | Branched Oak SRA - Area 2 Homestead

Total sites: 37, RV sites: 25, Elec sites: 25, Central water, Vault/pit toilet, No showers, No RV dump, Tents: $15/RVs: $25-30, $8 ($6 in-state residents) daily entrance fee, Stay limit: 14 days, Open all year, Reservations accepted, Elev: 1293ft/394m, Tel: 402-783-3400, Nearest town: Raymond. GPS: 40.961221, -96.894449

91 • C5 | Branched Oak SRA - Area 2 Homestead Equestrian

Total sites: 23, RV sites: 15, Elec sites: 15, Central water, Flush toilet, Free showers, RV dump, Tents: $20/RVs: $35, $8 ($6 in-state residents) daily entrance fee, Stay limit: 14 days, Open all year, Reservations accepted, Elev: 1292ft/394m, Tel: 402-783-3400, Nearest town: Raymond. GPS: 40.964306, -96.896999

92 • C5 | Branched Oak SRA - Area 3

Dispersed sites, Central water, Vault/pit toilet, Tent & RV camping: $10, $8 ($6 in-state residents) daily entrance fee, Stay limit: 14 days, Open all year, Elev: 1322ft/403m, Tel: 402-783-3400, Nearest town: Raymond. GPS: 40.971938, -96.896751

93 • C5 | Branched Oak SRA - Area 4 Middle Oak Creek

Total sites: 187, RV sites: 187, Elec sites: 159, Water at site, Flush toilet, Free showers, RV dump, Tents: $15/RVs: $15-30, $8 ($6 in-state residents) daily entrance fee, Stay limit: 14 days, Open all year, Reservations accepted, Elev: 1312ft/400m, Tel: 402-783-3400, Nearest town: Raymond. GPS: 40.971131, -96.887004

94 • C5 | Branched Oak SRA - Area 8

Dispersed sites, Central water, Vault/pit toilet, Tent & RV camping: $10, $8 ($6 in-state residents) daily entrance fee, Stay limit: 14 days, Open all year, Elev: 1280ft/390m, Tel: 402-783-3400, Nearest town: Raymond. GPS: 40.986772, -96.889893

95 • C5 | Conestoga Lake SRA

Total sites: 57, RV sites: 33, Elec sites: 25, Water at site, Vault/pit toilet, No showers, RV dump, Tents: $15/RVs: $25-30, $8 ($6 in-state residents) daily entrance fee, Stay limit: 14 days, Open all year, Reservations not accepted, Elev: 1257ft/383m, Tel: 402-796-2362, Nearest town: Denton. GPS: 40.771086, -96.851704

96 • C5 | Czechland RA - LPNNRD

Total sites: 11, RV sites: 11, Elec sites: 11, Central water, Vault/pit toilet, No showers, No RV dump, Tent & RV camping: Fee unk, Open all year, Elev: 1427ft/435m, Tel: 402-443-4675, Nearest town: Prague. GPS: 41.327798, -96.813317

97 • C5 | Elkhorn Crossing Rec Area - NNRD

Total sites: 17, RV sites: 8, Water available, Vault/pit toilet, Tent & RV camping: Free, Open Apr-Oct, Reservations not accepted, Elev: 1131ft/345m, Tel: 402-444-6222, Nearest town: Valley. GPS: 41.362201, -96.301965

98 • C5 | Kirkman's Cove RA - East Loop - NNRD

Total sites: 20, RV sites: 20, Elec sites: 16, Central water, Vault/pit toilet, No showers, No RV dump, Tent & RV camping: $12, Open all year, Elev: 1060ft/323m, Tel: 402-335-3325, Nearest town: Humboldt. GPS: 40.187866, -95.988656

99 • C5 | Kirkman's Cove RA - West Loop - NNRD

Total sites: 9, RV sites: 9, Central water, Vault/pit toilet, No showers, No RV dump, Tent & RV camping: $12, Open all year, Elev: 1063ft/324m, Tel: 402-335-3325, Nearest town: Humboldt. GPS: 40.184796, -95.992951

100 • C5 | Lake Wanahoo Park - RV Area

Total sites: 75, RV sites: 75, Elec sites: 75, Central water, Flush toilet, Free showers, No RV dump, Tent & RV camping: $15-19, $8 ($6 in-state residents) daily entrance fee, Open all year, Reservations accepted, Elev: 1201ft/366m, Tel: 402-443-1037, Nearest town: Wahoo. GPS: 41.243901, -96.617575

101 • C5 | Louisville Lakes SRA - Area 1

Total sites: 53, RV sites: 53, Elec sites: 53, Central water, Flush toilet, Free showers, RV dump, Tents: $15/RVs: $25-30, $8 ($6 in-state residents) daily entrance fee, Stay limit: 14 days, Open all year, Reservations accepted, Elev: 1037ft/316m, Tel: 402-234-6855, Nearest town: Louisville. GPS: 41.006753, -96.163588

102 • C5 | Louisville Lakes SRA - Area 2

Total sites: 76, RV sites: 76, Elec sites: 76, Central water, Flush toilet, Free showers, RV dump, Tent & RV camping: $25-30, $8 ($6 in-state residents) daily entrance fee, Stay limit: 14 days, Open all year, Reservations accepted, Elev: 1047ft/319m, Tel: 402-234-6855, Nearest town: Louisville. GPS: 41.003948, -96.171481

103 • C5 | Louisville Lakes SRA - Area 3

Total sites: 113, RV sites: 113, Elec sites: 100, Central water, Flush toilet, Free showers, RV dump, Tents: $15/RVs: $25-30, $8 ($6 in-state residents) daily entrance fee, Stay limit: 14 days, Open all year, Reservations accepted, Elev: 1037ft/316m, Tel: 402-234-6855, Nearest town: Louisville. GPS: 41.000815, -96.179045

104 • C5 | Memphis Lake SRA

Total sites: 100, RV sites: 100, Elec sites: 18, Central water, Vault/pit toilet, No showers, RV dump, Tents: $15/RVs: $30, $6 daily entrance fee, Stay limit: 14 days, Open all year, Reservations not accepted, Elev: 1129ft/344m, Tel: 402-471-5497, Nearest town: Memphis. GPS: 41.101699, -96.437418

105 • C5 | Olive Creek Lake SRA

Total sites: 50, RV sites: 50, Central water, Vault/pit toilet, No showers, No RV dump, Tent & RV camping: $15, $8 ($6 in-state residents) daily entrance fee, Stay limit: 14 days, Open all year, Reservations not accepted, Elev: 1316ft/401m, Tel: 402-796-2362, Nearest town: Kramer. GPS: 40.580566, -96.847900

106 • C5 | Pawnee SRA - Lakeview

Total sites: 78, RV sites: 73, Elec sites: 73, Water at site, Flush toilet, Free showers, RV dump, Tents: $15/RVs: $25-30, $8 ($6 in-state residents) daily entrance fee, Stay limit: 14 days, Open all year, Max Length: 53ft, Reservations accepted, Elev: 1257ft/383m, Tel: 402-796-2362, Nearest town: Emerald. GPS: 40.857994, -96.873697

107 • C5 | Pawnee SRA - West Superior RV

Total sites: 28, RV sites: 28, No water, Vault/pit toilet, RV dump, No tents/RVs: $15, $8 ($6 in-state residents) daily entrance fee, Stay limit: 14 days, Open all year, Elev: 1240ft/378m, Tel: 402-796-2362, Nearest town: Emerald. GPS: 40.857963, -96.890377

108 • C5 | Riverview Marina SRA

Total sites: 46, RV sites: 46, Elec sites: 16, Central water, Flush toilet, Free showers, No RV dump, Tents: $15/RVs: $25, $8 ($6 in-state residents) daily entrance fee, Stay limit: 14 days, Open all year, Reservations not accepted, Elev: 935ft/285m, Tel: 402-873-7222, Nearest town: Nebraska City. GPS: 40.692332, -95.849992

109 • C5 | Rockford SRA

Total sites: 72, RV sites: 32, Elec sites: 30, Water at site, Vault/pit toilet, No showers, No RV dump, Tents: $15/RVs: $25-30, $8 ($6 in-state residents) daily entrance fee, Stay limit: 14 days, Open all year, Reservations not accepted, Elev: 1371ft/418m, Tel: 402-729-5777, Nearest town: Beatrice. GPS: 40.227539, -96.580811

110 • C5 | Stage Coach Lake SRA

Total sites: 72, RV sites: 72, Elec sites: 22, Water at site, Vault/pit toilet, No showers, No RV dump, Tents: $15/RVs: $25-30, $8 ($6 in-state residents) daily entrance fee, Stay limit: 14 days, Open all year, Reservations not accepted, Elev: 1286ft/392m, Tel: 402-796-2362, Nearest town: Hickman. GPS: 40.599554, -96.647358

111 • C5 | Two Rivers SRA - Cottonwood

Total sites: 46, RV sites: 46, Elec sites: 46, Water at site, Flush toilet, Free showers, RV dump, Tent & RV camping: $30, $8 ($6 in-state residents) daily entrance fee, Stay limit: 14 days, Open all year, Max Length: 60ft, Reservations accepted, Elev: 1132ft/345m, Tel: 402-359-5165, Nearest town: Venice. GPS: 41.227806, -96.357956

112 • C5 | Two Rivers SRA - Fawn Meadows

Total sites: 12, RV sites: 12, Elec sites: 12, Central water, Flush toilet, Free showers, RV dump, Tent & RV camping: $30, $8 ($6 in-state residents) daily entrance fee, Stay limit: 14 days, Open all year, Max Length: 40ft, Reservations accepted, Elev: 1125ft/343m, Tel: 402-359-5165, Nearest town: Venice. GPS: 41.215433, -96.349315

113 • C5 | Two Rivers SRA - Goldenrod

Total sites: 45, RV sites: 45, Elec sites: 30, Water at site, Flush toilet, Free showers, RV dump, Tents: $15/RVs: $25-30, $8 ($6 in-state residents) daily entrance fee, Stay limit: 14 days, Open all year, Max Length: 50ft, Reservations accepted, Elev: 1122ft/342m, Tel: 402-359-5165, Nearest town: Venice. GPS: 41.225812, -96.352391

114 • C5 | Two Rivers SRA - Lakeside

Total sites: 36, RV sites: 36, Elec sites: 36, Water at site, Flush toilet, Free showers, RV dump, Tent & RV camping: $25-30, $8 ($6 in-state residents) daily entrance fee, Stay limit: 14 days, Open all year, Max Length: 50ft, Reservations accepted, Elev: 1116ft/340m, Tel: 402-359-5165, Nearest town: Venice. GPS: 41.215135, -96.348258

115 • C5 | Two Rivers SRA - Oak Grove

Total sites: 16, RV sites: 16, Elec sites: 16, Water at site, Flush toilet, Free showers, RV dump, Tent & RV camping: $25-30, $8 ($6 in-state residents) daily entrance fee, Stay limit: 14 days, Open all year, Max Length: 50ft, Reservations accepted, Elev: 1116ft/340m, Tel: 402-359-5165, Nearest town: Venice. GPS: 41.226971, -96.354955

116 • C5 | Two Rivers SRA - Riverside

Total sites: 37, RV sites: 37, Central water, RV dump, Tent & RV camping: $15, $8 ($6 in-state residents) daily entrance fee, Stay limit: 14 days, Open all year, Reservations accepted, Elev: 1119ft/341m, Tel: 402-359-5165, Nearest town: Venice. GPS: 41.220991, -96.357267

117 • C5 | Verdon Lake SRA

Total sites: 20, RV sites: 20, Central water, Vault/pit toilet, No showers, No RV dump, Tent & RV camping: $15, $8 ($6 in-state residents) daily entrance fee, Stay limit: 14 days, Open all year, Reservations not accepted, Elev: 946ft/288m, Tel: 402-883-2575, Nearest town: Verdon. GPS: 40.145697, -95.724472

118 • C5 | Wagon Train SRA

Total sites: 108, RV sites: 28, Elec sites: 28, Water at site, Vault/pit toilet, No showers, RV dump, Tents: $15/RVs: $25-30, $8 ($6 in-state residents) daily entrance fee, Stay limit: 14 days, Open all year, Reservations not accepted, Elev: 1299ft/396m, Tel: 402-796-2362, Nearest town: Hickman. GPS: 40.624386, -96.578158

Nevada

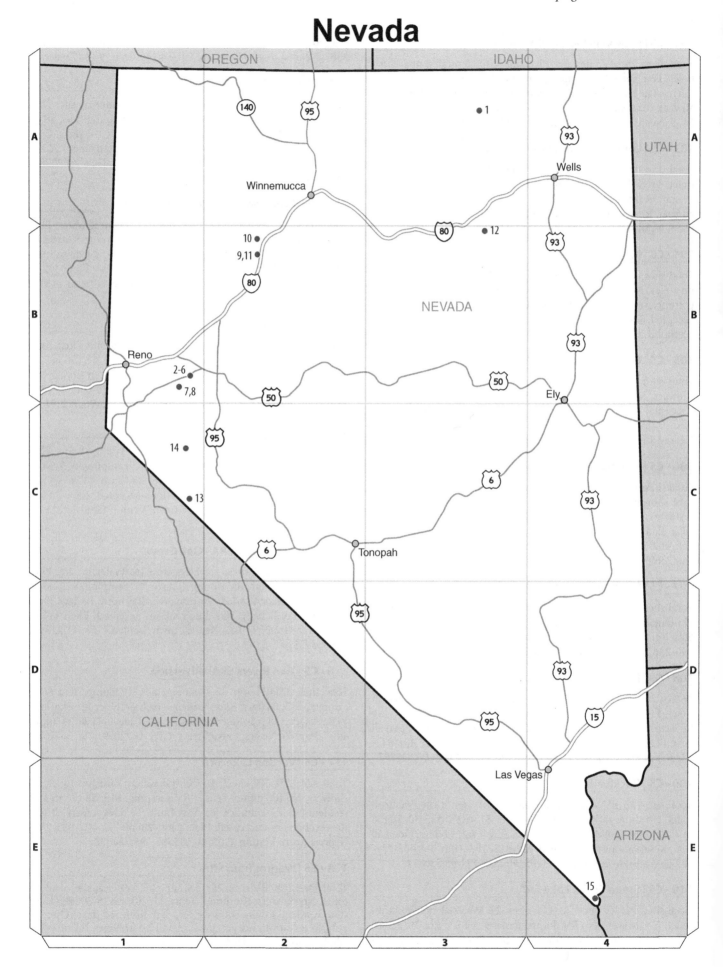

Map	ID	Map	ID
A3	1	B3	12
B1	2-8	C1	13-14
B2	9-11	E4	15

Alphabetical List of Camping Areas

1 • A3 | Wild Horse SRA

Total sites: 33, RV sites: 33, Central water, Flush toilet, Free showers, RV dump, Tent & RV camping: $15, Open all year, Max Length: 45ft, Elev: 6270ft/1911m, Tel: 775-385-5939, Nearest town: Mountain City. GPS: 41.669487, -115.799783

2 • B1 | Lahontan SRA - Blackbird Point

Dispersed sites, No water, Vault/pit toilet, Tent & RV camping: $15, Stay limit: 14 days, Elev: 4176ft/1273m, Tel: 775-867-3500, Nearest town: Fallon. GPS: 39.455211, -119.080357

3 • B1 | Lahontan SRA - Horseshoe Point

Dispersed sites, No water, Vault/pit toilet, Tent & RV camping: $15, Stay limit: 14 days, Elev: 4180ft/1274m, Tel: 775-867-3500, Nearest town: Fallon. GPS: 39.439665, -119.063344

4 • B1 | Lahontan SRA - LD Sites 1-11

Dispersed sites, No water, Vault/pit toilet, Tent & RV camping: $15, Stay limit: 14 days, Elev: 4193ft/1278m, Tel: 775-867-3500, Nearest town: Fallon. GPS: 39.446038, -119.047535

5 • B1 | Lahontan SRA - Overlook

Dispersed sites, No water, Vault/pit toilet, Tent & RV camping: $15, Stay limit: 14 days, Elev: 4193ft/1278m, Tel: 775-867-3500, Nearest town: Fallon. GPS: 39.463296, -119.070397

6 • B1 | Lahontan SRA - River Camp

Dispersed sites, Central water, Vault/pit toilet, No showers, RV dump, Tent & RV camping: $15, Stay limit: 14 days, Elev: 4078ft/1243m, Tel: 775-867-3500, Nearest town: Fallon. GPS: 39.464446, -119.061985

7 • B1 | Lahontan SRA - Silver Springs #7

Total sites: 21, RV sites: 21, Central water, Flush toilet, Free showers, RV dump, Tent & RV camping: $15, Stay limit: 14 days, Max Length: 60ft, Elev: 4170ft/1271m, Tel: 775-867-3500, Nearest town: Fallon. GPS: 39.377197, -119.188477

8 • B1 | Lahontan SRA - SS Sites 1-14

Dispersed sites, No water, Vault/pit toilet, Tent & RV camping: $15, Stay limit: 14 days, Elev: 4160ft/1268m, Tel: 775-867-3500, Nearest town: Fallon. GPS: 39.365728, -119.179422

9 • B2 | Rye Patch SRA - Dam

Total sites: 22, RV sites: 22, Central water, Flush toilet, No showers, RV dump, Tent & RV camping: $20, NV residents: $15, Stay limit: 14 days, Open all year, Max Length: 45ft, Elev: 4121ft/1256m, Tel: 775-538-7321, Nearest town: Lovelock. GPS: 40.466848, -118.307738

10 • B2 | Rye Patch SRA - Pit Taylor Cove

Dispersed sites, No water, Vault/pit toilet, Tent & RV camping: $15, Stay limit: 14 days, Open all year, Elev: 4160ft/1268m, Tel: 775-538-7321, Nearest town: Lovelock. GPS: 40.603098, -118.313131

11 • B2 | Rye Patch SRA - West Side

Total sites: 25, RV sites: 25, Central water, Flush toilet, Free showers, RV dump, Tent & RV camping: $15, Stay limit: 14 days, Open all year, Max Length: 45ft, Elev: 4147ft/1264m, Tel: 775-538-7321, Nearest town: Lovelock. GPS: 40.473071, -118.313414

12 • B3 | South Fork SRA

Total sites: 25, RV sites: 25, Central water, Flush toilet, Free showers, RV dump, Tent & RV camping: $15, Stay limit: 14 days, Open May-Oct, Max Length: 30ft, Elev: 5262ft/1604m, Tel: 775-744-4346, Nearest town: Elko. GPS: 40.676482, -115.753372

13 • C1 | Walker River SRA - Nine Mile Elbow - Bighorn

Dispersed sites, No water, No toilets, Tent & RV camping: $15, Stay limit: 14 days, Elev: 5650ft/1722m, Nearest town: Bridgeport (CA). GPS: 38.432624, -119.040831

14 • C1 | Walker River SRA - Riverbend

Total sites: 16, RV sites: 16, Central water, Flush toilet, Free showers, RV dump, Tent & RV camping: $15, Stay limit: 14 days, Reservations not accepted, Elev: 4533ft/1382m, Nearest town: Yerington. GPS: 38.851244, -119.092664

15 • E4 | Big Bend of Colorado RA

Total sites: 24, RV sites: 24, Elec sites: 24, Water at site, Flush toilet, Free showers, RV dump, Tent & RV camping: $30, 24 Full hookups, Stay limit: 14 days, Open all year, Max Length: 60ft, Reservations not accepted, Elev: 515ft/157m, Tel: 702-298-1859, Nearest town: Laughlin. GPS: 35.114154, -114.645573

New Jersey

CT

NEW YORK

A

287

80

80

Newark

78

1

95

287

B

PENNSYLVANIA

95

Trenton

195

C

295

Toms River

Garden State Pkwy

Atlantic Ocean

NEW JERSEY

D

MD

E

DELAWARE

Cape May

1   2   3   4

Map	ID	Map	ID
B2	1		

Alphabetical List of Camping Areas

1 • B2 | Spruce Run RA

Total sites: 67, RV sites: 67, Central water, Flush toilet, Free showers, No RV dump, Tent & RV camping: $25, NJ residents: $20, Open Apr-Oct, Reservations accepted, Elev: 272ft/83m, Tel: 908-638-8572, Nearest town: Clinton. GPS: 40.654717, -74.928704

New York

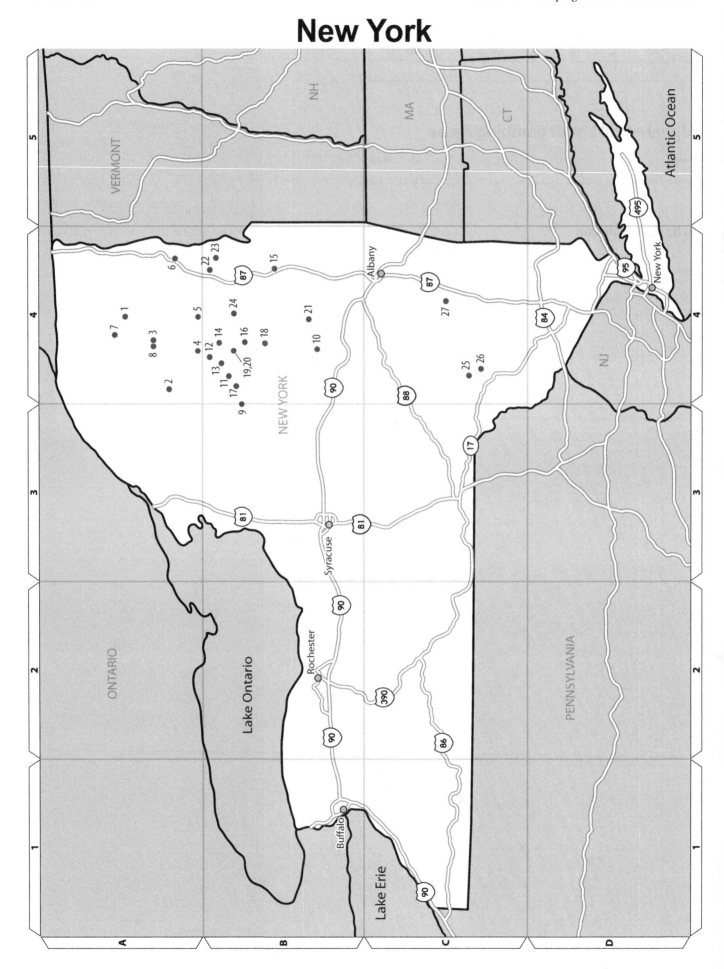

Map	ID	Map	ID
A4	1-8	B4	10-24
B3	9	C4	25-27

Alphabetical List of Camping Areas

1 • A4 | Buck Pond - NY DEC

Total sites: 116, RV sites: 116, Central water, Flush toilet, Free showers, RV dump, Tent & RV camping: $25, NY residents: $5 discount, Generator hours: 0900-1100/1600-1900, Open May-Sep, Reservations accepted, Elev: 1713ft/522m, Tel: 518-891-3449, Nearest town: Gabriels. GPS: 44.503418, -74.115967

2 • A4 | Cranberry Lake - DEC

Total sites: 173, RV sites: 173, Central water, Flush toilet, Free showers, RV dump, Tent & RV camping: $25, NY residents: $5 discount, Generator hours: 0900-1100/1600-1900, Open May-Oct, Reservations accepted, Elev: 1594ft/486m, Tel: 315-848-2315, Nearest town: Cranberry Lake. GPS: 44.199063, -74.825039

3 • A4 | Fish Creek Pond - DEC

Total sites: 355, RV sites: 355, Central water, Flush toilet, Pay showers, RV dump, Tent & RV camping: $27, NY residents: $5 discount, Generator hours: 0900-1100/1600-1900, Open Apr-Oct, Max Length: 40ft, Reservations accepted, Elev: 1608ft/490m, Tel: 518-891-4560, Nearest town: Saranac Lake. GPS: 44.304144, -74.358832

4 • A4 | Lake Eaton - DEC

Total sites: 135, RV sites: 135, Central water, Flush toilet, Free showers, RV dump, Tent & RV camping: $25, NY residents: $5 discount, Generator hours: 0900-1100/1600-1900, Open May-Oct, Reservations accepted, Elev: 1778ft/542m, Tel: 518-624-2641, Nearest town: Long Lake. GPS: 43.986109, -74.459432

5 • A4 | Lake Harris - DEC

Total sites: 89, RV sites: 89, Central water, Flush toilet, Free showers, RV dump, Tent & RV camping: $23, NY residents: $5 discount, Generator hours: 0900-1100/1600-1900, Open May-Sep, Reservations accepted, Elev: 1614ft/492m, Tel: 518-582-2503, Nearest town: Newcomb. GPS: 43.977899, -74.132361

6 • A4 | Lincoln Pond - DEC

Total sites: 35, RV sites: 35, Central water, Flush toilet, Free showers, RV dump, Tent & RV camping: $23, NY residents: $5 discount, Generator hours: 0900-1100/1600-1900, Open May-Sep, Reservations accepted, Elev: 1112ft/339m, Tel: 518-942-5292, Nearest town: Elizabethtown. GPS: 44.136475, -73.578369

7 • A4 | Meacham Lake - DEC

Total sites: 224, RV sites: 224, Central water, Flush toilet, Free showers, RV dump, Tent & RV camping: $25, NY residents: $5 discount, Generator hours: 0900-1100/1600-1900, Open May-Oct, Elev: 1591ft/485m, Tel: 518-483-5116, Nearest town: Duane. GPS: 44.578857, -74.286377

8 • A4 | Rollins Pond - DEC

Total sites: 287, RV sites: 287, Central water, Flush toilet, Free showers, RV dump, Tent & RV camping: $25, NY residents: $5 discount, Generator hours: 0900-1100/1600-1900, Open May-Sep, Max Length: 40ft, Reservations accepted, Elev: 1637ft/499m, Tel: 518-891-3239, Nearest town: Tupper Lake. GPS: 44.306152, -74.405029

9 • B3 | Nick's Lake - DEC

Total sites: 112, RV sites: 112, Central water, Flush toilet, Free showers, RV dump, Tent & RV camping: $27, NY residents: $5 discount, Generator hours: 0900-1100/1600-1900, Open May-Oct, Reservations accepted, Elev: 1775ft/541m, Tel: 315-369-3314, Nearest town: Old Forge. GPS: 43.682039, -74.984994

10 • B4 | Caroga Lake CG - NY DEC

Total sites: 161, RV sites: 161, Central water, Flush toilet, Free showers, RV dump, Tent & RV camping: $25, NY residents: $5 discount, Generator hours: 0900-1100/1600-1900, Open May-Sep, Reservations accepted, Elev: 1496ft/456m, Tel: 518-835-4241, Nearest town: Caroga Lake. GPS: 43.123291, -74.473389

11 • B4 | Eighth Lake CG - NY DEC

Total sites: 126, RV sites: 126, Central water, Flush toilet, Free showers, RV dump, Tent & RV camping: $27, NY residents: $5 discount, Generator hours: 0900-1100/1600-1900, Open May-Oct, Max Length: 40ft, Reservations accepted, Elev: 1782ft/543m, Tel: 315-354-4120, Nearest town: Imlet. GPS: 43.769028, -74.709628

12 • B4 | Forked Lake - DEC

Total sites: 80, RV sites: 3, No water, Vault/pit toilet, Tent & RV camping: $23, Most sites accessible by boat or trail only, NY residents: $5 discount, Generator hours: 0900-1100/1600-1900, Open May-Sep, Max Length: 20ft, Reservations accepted, Elev: 1778ft/542m, Tel: 518-624-6646, Nearest town: Long Lake. GPS: 43.906436, -74.526825

13 • B4 | Golden Beach - DEC

Total sites: 205, RV sites: 205, Central water, Flush toilet, Free showers, RV dump, Tent & RV camping: $25, NY residents: $5 discount, Generator hours: 0900-1100/1600-1900, Open May-Sep, Reservations accepted, Elev: 1798ft/548m, Tel: 315-354-4230, Nearest town: Raquette Lake. GPS: 43.817383, -74.597656

14 • B4 | Lake Durant - DEC

Total sites: 61, RV sites: 61, Central water, Flush toilet, Free showers, RV dump, Tent & RV camping: $25, NY residents: $5 discount, Generator hours: 0900-1100/1600-1900, Open May-Oct, Reservations accepted, Elev: 1772ft/540m, Tel: 518-352-7797, Nearest town: Blue Mountain Lake. GPS: 43.838063, -74.390583

15 • B4 | Lake George Battleground - DEC

Total sites: 68, RV sites: 68, Central water, Flush toilet, Free showers, RV dump, Tent & RV camping: $27, NY residents: $5 discount, Generator hours: 0900-1100/1600-1900, Open May-Oct, Reservations accepted, Elev: 387ft/118m, Tel: 518-668-3348, Nearest town: Lake George Village. GPS: 43.416016, -73.708008

16 • B4 | Lewey Lake - DEC

Total sites: 207, RV sites: 207, Central water, Flush toilet, Free showers, RV dump, Tent & RV camping: $25, NY residents: $5 discount, Generator hours: 0900-1100/1600-1900, Open May-Oct, Reservations accepted, Elev: 1706ft/520m, Tel: 518-648-5266, Nearest town: Lake Pleasant. GPS: 43.649919, -74.389047

17 • B4 | Limekiln Lake - DEC

Total sites: 271, RV sites: 271, Central water, Flush toilet, Free showers, RV dump, Tent & RV camping: $25, NY residents: $5 discount, Generator hours: 0900-1100/1600-1900, Open May-Sep, Reservations accepted, Elev: 1936ft/590m, Tel: 315-357-4401, Nearest town: Inlet. GPS: 43.718811, -74.811741

18 • B4 | Moffitt Beach - DEC

Total sites: 261, RV sites: 261, Central water, Flush toilet, Free showers, RV dump, Tent & RV camping: $27, NY residents: $5 discount, Generator hours: 0900-1100/1600-1900, Open May-Oct, Reservations accepted, Elev: 1824ft/556m, Tel: 518-548-7102, Nearest town: Speculator. GPS: 43.492936, -74.401036

19 • B4 | Moose River Plains - Cedar River Flow - DEC

Total sites: 8, RV sites: 7, No water, No toilets, Tent & RV camping: Free, Winter access by foot or snowmobile, Open all year, Elev: 2116ft/645m, Tel: 518-863-4545, Nearest town: Indian Lake. GPS: 43.726296, -74.473356

20 • B4 | Moose River Plains - Wakely Pond- DEC

Dispersed sites, No toilets, Tent & RV camping: Free, Winter access by foot or snowmobile, Open all year, Elev: 2129ft/649m, Tel: 518-863-4545, Nearest town: Indian Lake. GPS: 43.737941, -74.464119

21 • B4 | Northampton Beach - DEC

Total sites: 224, RV sites: 224, Central water, Flush toilet, Free showers, RV dump, Tent & RV camping: $27, NY residents: $5 discount, Generator hours: 0900-1100/1600-1900, Open May-Oct, Reservations accepted, Elev: 804ft/245m, Tel: 518-863-6000, Nearest town: Northville. GPS: 43.183350, -74.174316

22 • B4 | Paradox Lake - DEC

Total sites: 58, RV sites: 58, Central water, Flush toilet, Free showers, RV dump, Tent & RV camping: $23, NY residents: $5 discount, Open May-Sep, Reservations accepted, Elev: 873ft/266m, Tel: 518-532-7451, Nearest town: Paradox. GPS: 43.885986, -73.681641

23 • B4 | Putnam Pond - DEC

Total sites: 72, RV sites: 63, Central water, Flush toilet, Free showers, RV dump, Tent & RV camping: $23, NY residents: $5 discount, Generator hours: 0900-1100/1600-1900, Open May-Oct, Reservations accepted, Elev: 1358ft/414m, Tel: 518-585-7280, Nearest town: Ticonderoga. GPS: 43.840099, -73.571764

24 • B4 | Siamese Ponds Wilderness - Thirteenth Lake - DEC

Dispersed sites, No toilets, Tent & RV camping: Free, Elev: 1719ft/524m, Nearest town: Johnsburg. GPS: 43.718602, -74.118388

25 • C4 | Little Pond - DEC

Total sites: 67, RV sites: 67, Central water, Flush toilet, Free showers, RV dump, Tent & RV camping: $27, NY residents: $5 discount, Generator hours: 0900-1100/1600-1900, Open May-Oct, Reservations accepted, Elev: 1993ft/607m, Tel: 845-439-5480, Nearest town: Margaretville. GPS: 42.037719, -74.743596

26 • C4 | Mongaup Pond - DEC

Total sites: 163, RV sites: 163, Central water, Flush toilet, Free showers, RV dump, Tent & RV camping: $27, NY residents: $5 discount, Generator hours: 0900-1100/1600-1900, Open May-Oct, Reservations accepted, Elev: 2146ft/654m, Tel: 845-439-4233, Nearest town: DeBruce. GPS: 41.958316, -74.690487

27 • C4 | North-South Lake - DEC

Total sites: 219, RV sites: 219, Central water, Flush toilet, Free showers, RV dump, Tent & RV camping: $27, NY residents: $5 discount, Generator hours: 0900-1100/1600-1900, Open May-Oct, Reservations accepted, Elev: 2175ft/663m, Tel: 518-589-5058, Nearest town: Haines Falls. GPS: 42.201548, -74.040676

North Carolina

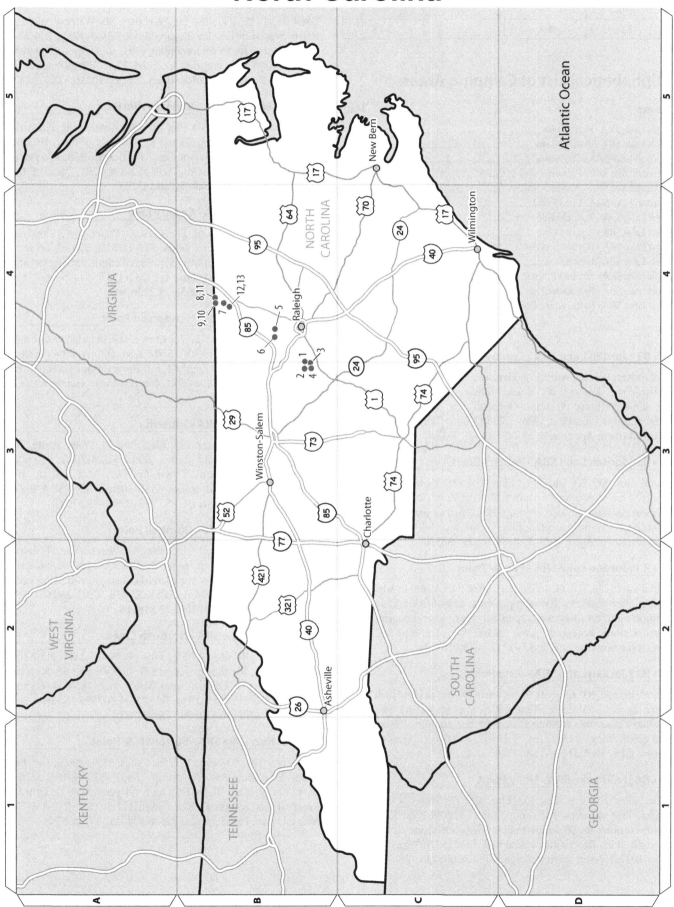

Map	ID	Map	ID
B3	1-4	B4	5-13

Alphabetical List of Camping Areas

1 • B3 | Jordan Lake SRA - Crosswinds

Total sites: 176, RV sites: 176, Elec sites: 129, Central water, Flush toilet, Free showers, RV dump, Tent & RV camping: $20-25, $6 senior/military discount, Open all year, Max Length: 140ft, Reservations accepted, Elev: 236ft/72m, Tel: 919-362-0586, Nearest town: Apex. GPS: 35.743153, -78.993732

2 • B3 | Jordan Lake SRA - Parkers Creek

Total sites: 247, RV sites: 247, Elec sites: 118, Water at site, Flush toilet, Free showers, RV dump, Tents: $19-48/RVs: $24-62, $6 senior/military discount, 6 group sites, Open all year, Max Length: 90ft, Reservations accepted, Elev: 249ft/76m, Tel: 919-362-0586, Nearest town: Apex. GPS: 35.748779, -79.038330

3 • B3 | Jordan Lake SRA - Poplar Point

Total sites: 578, RV sites: 578, Elec sites: 343, Water at site, Flush toilet, Free showers, RV dump, Tents: $19-48/RVs: $24-62, $6 senior/military discount, Open all year, Max Length: 130ft, Reservations accepted, Elev: 308ft/94m, Tel: 919-362-0586, Nearest town: Apex. GPS: 35.724121, -79.016113

4 • B3 | Jordan Lake SRA - Vista Point

Total sites: 50, RV sites: 50, Elec sites: 50, Water at site, Flush toilet, Free showers, RV dump, Tent & RV camping: $24-62, $6 senior/military discount, 5 group sites, Max Length: 40ft, Reservations accepted, Elev: 233ft/71m, Tel: 919-362-0586, Nearest town: Apex. GPS: 35.703166, -79.051149

5 • B4 | Falls Lake SRA - Holly Point

Total sites: 153, RV sites: 153, Elec sites: 89, Water at site, Flush toilet, Free showers, RV dump, Tents: $19-49/RVs: $24-62, $6 daily entrance fee $6 senior/military discount, Open all year, Max Length: 95ft, Reservations accepted, Elev: 322ft/98m, Tel: 919-676-1027, Nearest town: Raleigh. GPS: 36.008233, -78.654449

6 • B4 | Falls Lake SRA - Rolling View

Total sites: 115, RV sites: 80, Elec sites: 80, Water at site, Flush toilet, Free showers, RV dump, Tents: $19-50/RVs: $24-63, $6 daily entrance fee $6 senior/military discount, Open all year, Max Length: 100ft, Reservations accepted, Elev: 312ft/95m, Tel: 919-676-1027, Nearest town: Raleigh. GPS: 36.010326, -78.726322

7 • B4 | Kerr Lake SRA - Bullocksville Park

Total sites: 64, RV sites: 64, Elec sites: 31, Water at site, Flush toilet, Free showers, RV dump, Tents: $23-48/RVs: $30-62, $6 senior/military discount, Open Apr-Sep, Max Length: 85ft, Reservations accepted, Elev: 312ft/95m, Tel: 252-438-7791, Nearest town: Henderson. GPS: 36.462473, -78.367793

8 • B4 | Kerr Lake SRA - County Line

Total sites: 61, RV sites: 61, Elec sites: 35, Water at site, Flush toilet, Free showers, RV dump, Tents: $23-48/RVs: $30-62, $6 senior/military discount, Open Apr-Sep, Max Length: 85ft, Reservations accepted, Elev: 348ft/106m, Tel: 252-438-7791, Nearest town: Henderson. GPS: 36.526855, -78.315674

9 • B4 | Kerr Lake SRA - Henderson Point

Total sites: 72, RV sites: 72, Elec sites: 43, Flush toilet, Free showers, RV dump, Tents: $23-48/RVs: $30-62, $6 senior/military discount, Open Apr-Sep, Max Length: 123ft, Reservations accepted, Elev: 361ft/110m, Tel: 252-438-7791, Nearest town: Henderson. GPS: 36.534642, -78.354846

10 • B4 | Kerr Lake SRA - Hibernia

Total sites: 143, RV sites: 143, Elec sites: 34, Water at site, Flush toilet, Free showers, RV dump, Tents: $23-48/RVs: $30-62, $6 senior/military discount, Open Apr-Oct, Max Length: 100ft, Reservations accepted, Elev: 335ft/102m, Tel: 252-438-7791, Nearest town: Henderson. GPS: 36.510986, -78.370850

11 • B4 | Kerr Lake SRA - Kimball Point

Total sites: 77, RV sites: 77, Elec sites: 47, Water at site, Flush toilet, Free showers, RV dump, Tents: $23-48/RVs: $30-62, $6 senior/military discount, Open Apr-Oct, Max Length: 90ft, Reservations accepted, Elev: 315ft/96m, Tel: 252-438-7791, Nearest town: Henderson. GPS: 36.541016, -78.318115

12 • B4 | Kerr Lake SRA - Nutbush Creek

Total sites: 80, RV sites: 80, Elec sites: 60, Water at site, Flush toilet, Free showers, RV dump, Tents: $23-48/RVs: $30-62, $6 senior/military discount, Open all year, Max Length: 80ft, Reservations accepted, Elev: 344ft/105m, Tel: 252-438-7791, Nearest town: Henderson. GPS: 36.412598, -78.397705

13 • B4 | Kerr Lake SRA - Satterwhite Point

Total sites: 115, RV sites: 115, Elec sites: 61, Water at site, Flush toilet, Free showers, RV dump, Tents: $23-48/RVs: $30-62, $6 senior/military discount, Open all year, Max Length: 90ft, Reservations accepted, Elev: 364ft/111m, Tel: 252-438-7791, Nearest town: Henderson. GPS: 36.434715, -78.369694

North Dakota

MINNESOTA

MANITOBA

SASKATCHEWAN

SOUTH DAKOTA

NORTH DAKOTA

MT

29

29

29

94

94

94

94

5

5

5

5

5

2

2

2

2

2

281

281

281

281

52

52

52

52

83

83

83

83

85

85

85

85

12

12

12

Grand Forks

Fargo

Jamestown

Bismarck

Minot

Williston

● 1

● 2

● 3

● 4

Map	ID	Map	ID
A3	1	C3	3
B2	2	D2	4

Alphabetical List of Camping Areas

1 • A3 | Carbury Recreation Area

Total sites: 10, RV sites: 10, Elec sites: 10, Tent & RV camping: Fee unk, Elev: 1624ft/495m, Tel: 701-228-2225, Nearest town: Bottineau. GPS: 48.877152, -100.551809

2 • B2 | Indian Hills SRA

Total sites: 70, RV sites: 61, Elec sites: 61, Flush toilet, Free showers, RV dump, Tents: $20/RVs: $20-30, 18 Full hookups, Concession, Open May-Oct, Reservations accepted, Elev: 1955ft/596m, Nearest town: White Shield. GPS: 47.607124, -102.100317

3 • C3 | Kimball Bottoms OHV - ND PRD

Dispersed sites, Vault/pit toilet, Tent & RV camping: Free, Elev: 1627ft/496m, Tel: 701-328-5357, Nearest town: Bismarck. GPS: 46.667844, -100.732906

4 • D2 | Sheep Creek Dam SRA

Total sites: 10, RV sites: 5, Elec sites: 5, Central water, Vault/pit toilet, No RV dump, Tent & RV camping: Donation, Stay limit: 5 days, Reservations not accepted, Elev: 2224ft/678m, Tel: 701-584-2354, Nearest town: Elgin. GPS: 46.338050, -101.848810

Oregon

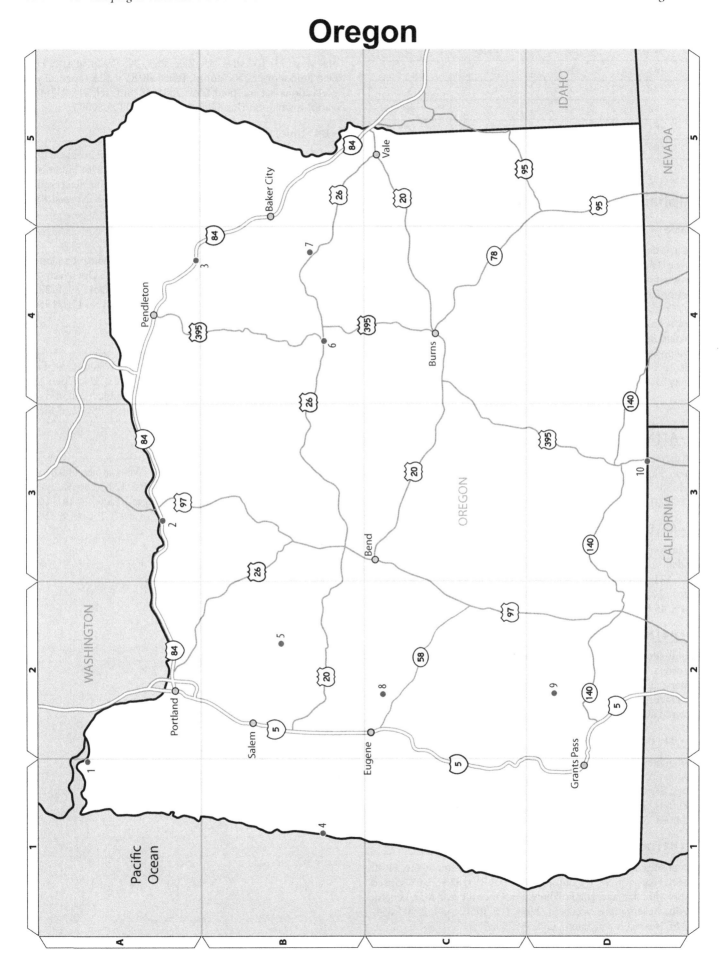

Map	ID	Map	ID
A1	1	B4	6-7
A3	2	C2	8
A4	3	D2	9
B1	4	D3	10
B2	5		

Alphabetical List of Camping Areas

1 • A1 | Nicolai Mtn OHV Area - Shingle Mill - ODF

Dispersed sites, No water, Vault/pit toilet, Tent & RV camping: Free, Staging Area, Reservations not accepted, Elev: 992ft/302m, Tel: 503-325-5451, Nearest town: Clatskanie. GPS: 46.150815, -123.452101

2 • A3 | Deschutes River SRA

Total sites: 59, RV sites: 59, Elec sites: 34, Central water, Flush toilet, Free showers, No RV dump, Tents: $10/RVs: $24, Group site: $71, Open all year, Max Length: 50ft, Reservations accepted, Elev: 243ft/74m, Tel: 541-739-2322, Nearest town: The Dalles. GPS: 45.632080, -120.908447

3 • A4 | Hilgard Junction SRA

Total sites: 17, RV sites: 17, Central water, Vault/pit toilet, No showers, No RV dump, Tent & RV camping: $10, Right beside interstate highway, Open Apr-Oct, Max Length: 30ft, Reservations not accepted, Elev: 3028ft/923m, Tel: 800-551-6949, Nearest town: LaGrande. GPS: 45.341713, -118.234019

4 • B1 | Beachside SRA

Total sites: 74, RV sites: 32, Elec sites: 32, Central water, Flush toilet, Free showers, RV dump, Tents: $21/RVs: $31, Hiker/biker sites: $8, Open Mar-Oct, Reservations accepted, Elev: 33ft/10m, Tel: 541-563-3220, Nearest town: Waldport. GPS: 44.381057, -124.088557

5 • B2 | Detroit Lake SRA

Total sites: 271, RV sites: 178, Elec sites: 175, Water at site, Flush toilet, Free showers, RV dump, Tents: $19/RVs: $28-33, CG closed UFN - fire damage, 107 Full hookups, Open all year, Max Length: 175ft, Reservations accepted, Elev: 1657ft/505m, Tel: 503-854-3346, Nearest town: Salem. GPS: 44.730651, -122.175511

6 • B4 | Clyde Holiday SRA

Total sites: 31, RV sites: 31, Elec sites: 31, Water at site, Flush toilet, Free showers, RV dump, Tents: $8/RVs: $26, Open all year, Reservations not accepted, Elev: 2881ft/878m, Tel: 541-932-4453, Nearest town: John Day. GPS: 44.416543, -119.089093

7 • B4 | Unity Lake SRA

Total sites: 35, RV sites: 35, Elec sites: 35, Water at site, Flush toilet, Free showers, RV dump, Tent & RV camping: $26, Hiker/biker sites: $8/person, Open Apr-Oct, Max Length: 40ft, Reservations accepted, Elev: 3848ft/1173m, Tel: 541-932-4453, Nearest town: John Day. GPS: 44.499133, -118.186874

8 • C2 | Fall Creek SRA - Cascara

Total sites: 39, RV sites: 39, Central water, Vault/pit toilet, No showers, No RV dump, Tent & RV camping: $19, Open May-Sep, Max Length: 45ft, Reservations not accepted, Elev: 892ft/272m, Tel: 541-937-1080, Nearest town: Eugene. GPS: 43.971914, -122.666625

9 • D2 | Joseph Stewart SRA

Total sites: 201, RV sites: 151, Elec sites: 151, Water at site, Flush toilet, Free showers, RV dump, Tents: $17/RVs: $24, Open Mar-Oct, Max Length: 80ft, Reservations accepted, Elev: 2005ft/611m, Tel: 541-560-3334, Nearest town: Medford. GPS: 42.684326, -122.614990

10 • D3 | Goose Lake SRA

Total sites: 47, RV sites: 47, Elec sites: 47, Water at site, Flush toilet, Free showers, RV dump, Tents: $17/RVs: $24, Open May-Sep, Max Length: 50ft, Reservations not accepted, Elev: 4744ft/1446m, Tel: 541-947-3111, Nearest town: Lakeview. GPS: 41.994246, -120.322344

South Carolina

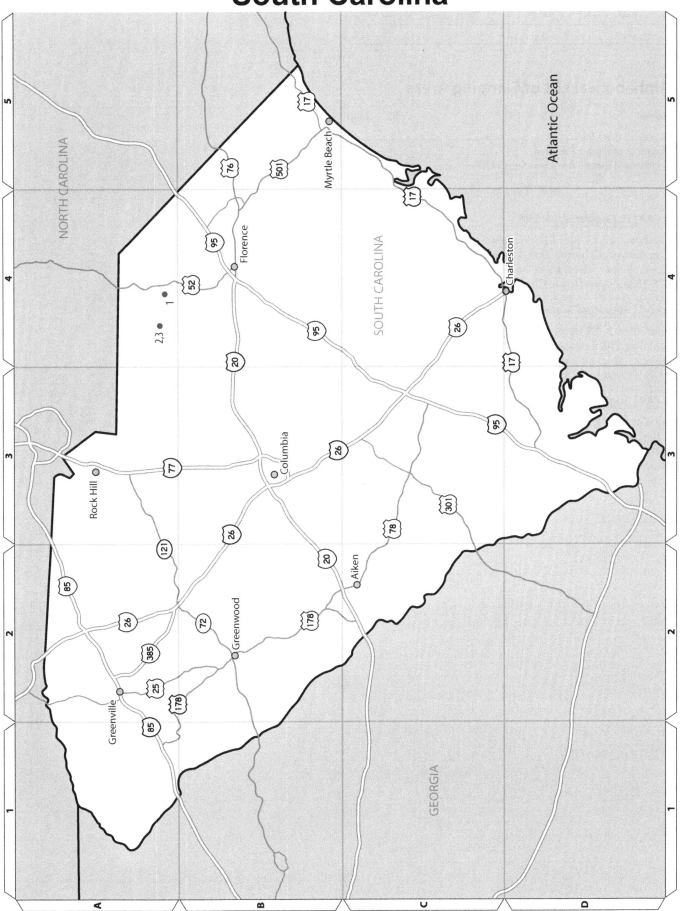

Map	ID	Map	ID
A4	1-3		

Alphabetical List of Camping Areas

1 • A4 | H. Cooper Black SRA

Total sites: 27, RV sites: 27, Elec sites: 27, Water at site, Flush toilet, Free showers, RV dump, Tent & RV camping: $16, Equestrian sites, Open all year, Reservations accepted, Elev: 269ft/82m, Tel: 843-378-1555, Nearest town: Cheraw. GPS: 34.562097, -79.928032

2 • A4 | Sugarloaf Mountain Rec Area

Total sites: 8, RV sites: 8, No water, Vault/pit toilet, Tent & RV camping: $10, 8 equestrian sites in area, Only 1 vault toilet, Open all year, Reservations required, Elev: 282ft/86m, Tel: 843-498-6478, Nearest town: Patrick. GPS: 34.587005, -80.127973

3 • A4 | Sugarloaf Mountain Rec Area - Sites 1A,1B

Total sites: 8, RV sites: 8, No water, Tent & RV camping: $10-15, 8 sites along road - 6 with shelters, Open all year, Max Length: 18ft, Reservations required, Elev: 313ft/95m, Tel: 843-498-6478, Nearest town: Patrick. GPS: 34.589949, -80.123354

South Dakota

MN

IA

25

29

44

26,27

47

Watertown

Sioux Falls

54,60

10 9

30 29

14

45,46

81

55,58,59

56,57

12

28

53

22

90

Aberdeen

Mitchell

52

281

48

8

50,51

7

49

23,24

42,43

40 41

39

Highmore

38

5

83

90

6

21

13,14

Mobridge 3,4

212

83

12,18

16,17

NEBRASKA

12

Murdo

83

15

14

Dupree

90

212

SOUTH DAKOTA

NORTH DAKOTA

2 1

90

212

Buffalo

85

79

11

Spearfish

Rapid City

31-37

18

MT

WY

A   B   C   D

Map	ID	Map	ID
A2	1-2	B5	25-30
A3	3-6	C1	31-37
A4	7-8	C3	38
A5	9-10	C4	39-43
B1	11	C5	44-47
B3	12-21	D4	48-53
B4	22-24	D5	54-60

Alphabetical List of Camping Areas

1 • A2 | Llewellyn Johns SRA

Total sites: 10, RV sites: 10, Elec sites: 10, Central water, Vault/pit toilet, No showers, No RV dump, Tent & RV camping: $15, No water Oct-Apr, Plus $8 daily entrance fee, Open all year, Reservations accepted, Elev: 2264ft/690m, Tel: 605-374-5114, Nearest town: Lemmon. GPS: 45.774052, -102.178441

2 • A2 | Shadehill SRA

Total sites: 56, RV sites: 56, Elec sites: 56, Central water, Flush toilet, Free showers, RV dump, Tent & RV camping: $28, Also cabins, Plus $8 daily entrance fee, Open May-Oct, Max Length: 80ft, Reservations accepted, Elev: 2297ft/700m, Tel: 605-374-5114, Nearest town: Lemmon. GPS: 45.763974, -102.233792

3 • A3 | Indian Creek SRA - CG A

Total sites: 80, RV sites: 80, Elec sites: 80, Central water, Flush toilet, Free showers, RV dump, Tent & RV camping: $20, Also cabins, Plus $8 daily entrance fee, Open all year, Reservations accepted, Elev: 1640ft/500m, Tel: 605-845-7112, Nearest town: Mobridge. GPS: 45.515169, -100.382683

4 • A3 | Indian Creek SRA - CG B

Total sites: 44, RV sites: 42, Elec sites: 42, Central water, Flush toilet, Free showers, RV dump, Tent & RV camping: $20, Plus $8 daily entrance fee, Open all year, Reservations accepted, Elev: 1637ft/499m, Tel: 605-845-7112, Nearest town: Mobridge. GPS: 45.517743, -100.390968

5 • A3 | Lake Hiddenwood SRA

Total sites: 13, RV sites: 13, Elec sites: 5, Central water, Vault/pit toilet, No showers, No RV dump, Tents: $11/RVs: $15, Plus $8 daily entrance fee, Open all year, Reservations accepted, Elev: 1795ft/547m, Tel: 605-845-7112, Nearest town: Selby. GPS: 45.545341, -99.976593

6 • A3 | West Pollock SRA

Total sites: 29, RV sites: 29, Elec sites: 29, Central water, Flush toilet, Free showers, RV dump, Tent & RV camping: $20, Plus $8 daily entrance fee, Open all year, Reservations accepted, Elev: 1637ft/499m, Tel: 605-845-7112, Nearest town: Pollock. GPS: 45.882085, -100.337348

7 • A4 | Mina Lake SRA

Total sites: 37, RV sites: 37, Elec sites: 37, Central water, Flush toilet, Free showers, RV dump, Tent & RV camping: $26, Plus $8 daily entrance fee, Open all year, Reservations accepted, Elev: 1424ft/434m, Tel: 605-626-3488, Nearest town: Aberdeen. GPS: 45.443964, -98.744582

8 • A4 | Richmond Lake SRA

Total sites: 24, RV sites: 24, Elec sites: 22, Central water, Flush toilet, Free showers, RV dump, Tents: $22/RVs: $22-26, Also cabins, Plus $8 daily entrance fee, Open all year, Reservations accepted, Elev: 1384ft/422m, Tel: 605-626-3488, Nearest town: Aberdeen. GPS: 45.533955, -98.620037

9 • A5 | Pickerel Lake East SRA

Total sites: 31, RV sites: 31, Elec sites: 31, Central water, Flush toilet, Free showers, RV dump, Tent & RV camping: $26, Also cabins, Plus $8 daily entrance fee, Open all year, Reservations accepted, Elev: 1886ft/575m, Tel: 605-486-4753, Nearest town: Waubay. GPS: 45.485613, -97.261666

10 • A5 | Pickerel Lake West SRA

Total sites: 41, RV sites: 41, Elec sites: 41, Central water, Flush toilet, Free showers, RV dump, Tent & RV camping: $26, Also cabins, Plus $8 daily entrance fee, Open all year, Reservations accepted, Elev: 1857ft/566m, Tel: 605-486-4753, Nearest town: Waubay. GPS: 45.502559, -97.280049

11 • B1 | Rocky Point SRA

Total sites: 66, RV sites: 66, Elec sites: 66, Central water, Flush toilet, Free showers, RV dump, Tent & RV camping: $26, Also cabins, Plus $8 daily entrance fee, Open all year, Reservations accepted, Elev: 2979ft/908m, Tel: 605-641-0023, Nearest town: Belle Fourche. GPS: 44.721501, -103.704484

12 • B3 | Cow Creek SRA

Total sites: 39, RV sites: 30, Elec sites: 30, Central water, Flush toilet, Free showers, No RV dump, Tents: $16/RVs: $20, Also cabins, Plus $8 daily entrance fee, Open all year, Reservations accepted, Elev: 1614ft/492m, Tel: 605-223-7722, Nearest town: Pierre. GPS: 44.557698, -100.479572

13 • B3 | Farm Island SRA - East

Total sites: 20, RV sites: 20, Elec sites: 20, Central water, Flush toilet, Free showers, RV dump, Tent & RV camping: $26, Open all year, Reservations accepted, Elev: 1430ft/436m, Tel: 605-773-2885, Nearest town: Pierre. GPS: 44.343827, -100.263466

14 • B3 | Farm Island SRA - Main

Total sites: 70, RV sites: 70, Elec sites: 70, Central water, Flush toilet, Free showers, RV dump, Tent & RV camping: $26, Also cabins, Open all year, Reservations accepted, Elev: 1424ft/434m, Tel: 605-773-2885, Nearest town: Pierre. GPS: 44.342147, -100.275185

15 • B3 | Little Moreau SRA

Total sites: 5, RV sites: 5, No water, Vault/pit toilet, Tent & RV camping: $15, Open all year, Reservations not accepted, Elev: 2023ft/617m, Tel: 605-374-5114, Nearest town: Timber Lake. GPS: 45.344397, -101.083395

16 • B3 | Oahe Downstream SRA - CG 3

Total sites: 42, RV sites: 42, Elec sites: 42, Central water, Flush toilet, Free showers, RV dump, Tent & RV camping: $23, Also cabins, Open Mar-Nov, Reservations accepted, Elev: 1424ft/434m, Tel: 605-223-7722, Nearest town: Ft. Pierre. GPS: 44.423768, -100.387725

17 • B3 | Oahe Downstream SRA - CG's 1,2

Total sites: 130, RV sites: 130, Elec sites: 130, Central water, Flush toilet, Free showers, RV dump, Tent & RV camping: $23, Plus $8 daily entrance fee, Open Mar-Nov, Reservations accepted, Elev: 1453ft/443m, Tel: 605-223-7722, Nearest town: Ft. Pierre. GPS: 44.433275, -100.390158

18 • B3 | Okobojo Point SRA

Total sites: 17, RV sites: 13, Central water, Flush toilet, Free showers, No RV dump, Tent & RV camping: $16, Plus $8 daily entrance fee, Open all year, Reservations not accepted, Elev: 1611ft/491m, Tel: 605-223-7722, Nearest town: Pierre. GPS: 44.568483, -100.504551

19 • B3 | Swan Creek SRA - East CG

Total sites: 8, RV sites: 8, Elec sites: 8, No water, Vault/pit toilet, Tent & RV camping: $20, Plus $8 daily entrance fee, Open all year, Reservations accepted, Elev: 1634ft/498m, Tel: 605-765-9410, Nearest town: Akaska. GPS: 45.317508, -100.260509

20 • B3 | Swan Creek SRA - West CG

Total sites: 15, RV sites: 15, Elec sites: 15, Central water, No toilets, No showers, RV dump, Tent & RV camping: $20, Plus $8 daily entrance fee, Open all year, Reservations accepted, Elev: 1621ft/494m, Tel: 605-765-9410, Nearest town: Akaska. GPS: 45.319558, -100.267196

21 • B3 | West Whitlock SRA

Total sites: 105, RV sites: 105, Elec sites: 105, Central water, Flush toilet, Free showers, RV dump, Tent & RV camping: $20, Also cabins, Plus $8 daily entrance fee, Open all year, Reservations accepted, Elev: 1637ft/499m, Tel: 605-765-9410, Nearest town: Gettysburg. GPS: 45.043213, -100.262207

22 • B4 | Amsden Lake SRA

Total sites: 11, RV sites: 11, Central water, Vault/pit toilet, No showers, No RV dump, Tent & RV camping: $15, Open all year, Elev: 1436ft/438m, Nearest town: Groton. GPS: 45.356295, -97.965074

23 • B4 | Lake Louise SRA - Main

Total sites: 29, RV sites: 29, Elec sites: 29, Central water, Flush toilet, Free showers, RV dump, Tent & RV camping: $26, Plus $8 daily entrance fee, Open all year, Reservations accepted, Elev: 1565ft/477m, Tel: 605-853-2533, Nearest town: Miller. GPS: 44.622249, -99.131702

24 • B4 | Lake Louise SRA - West

Total sites: 10, RV sites: 10, No water, Vault/pit toilet, Tent & RV camping: $22, Plus $8 daily entrance fee, Reservations not accepted, Elev: 1572ft/479m, Tel: 605-853-2533, Nearest town: Miller. GPS: 44.623719, -99.147756

25 • B5 | Lake Cochrane SRA

Total sites: 30, RV sites: 30, Elec sites: 30, Central water, Flush toilet, Free showers, RV dump, Tent & RV camping: $26, Plus $8 daily entrance fee, Open all year, Reservations accepted, Elev: 1686ft/514m, Tel: 605-882-5200, Nearest town: Clear Lake. GPS: 44.713697, -96.478476

26 • B5 | Lake Poinsett SRA - CG 1

Total sites: 83, RV sites: 77, Elec sites: 77, Central water, Flush toilet, Free showers, RV dump, Tent & RV camping: $26, Plus $8 daily entrance fee, Open all year, Reservations accepted, Elev: 1654ft/504m, Tel: 605-983-5085, Nearest town: Arlington. GPS: 44.536773, -97.081495

27 • B5 | Lake Poinsett SRA - CG 2

Total sites: 25, RV sites: 25, Elec sites: 25, Central water, Flush toilet, Free showers, RV dump, Tent & RV camping: $26, Plus $8 daily entrance fee, Open all year, Reservations accepted, Elev: 1670ft/509m, Tel: 605-983-5085, Nearest town: Arlington. GPS: 44.538422, -97.072108

28 • B5 | Lake Thompson SRA

Total sites: 103, RV sites: 97, Elec sites: 97, Central water, Flush toilet, Free showers, RV dump, Tents: $22/RVs: $26, Plus $8 daily entrance fee, Open all year, Reservations accepted, Elev: 1719ft/524m, Tel: 605-847-4893, Nearest town: Lake Preston. GPS: 44.321385, -97.432967

29 • B5 | Pelican Lake SRA

Total sites: 82, RV sites: 82, Elec sites: 82, Central water, Flush toilet, Free showers, RV dump, Tent & RV camping: $26, Includes 6 horse sites, Plus $8 daily entrance fee, Open all year, Reservations accepted, Elev: 1716ft/523m, Tel: 605-882-5200, Nearest town: Watertown. GPS: 44.856571, -97.201738

30 • B5 | Sandy Shore SRA

Total sites: 23, RV sites: 15, Elec sites: 15, Central water, Flush toilet, Free showers, No RV dump, Tents: $22/RVs: $22-26, Plus $8 daily entrance fee, Open all year, Reservations accepted, Elev: 1719ft/524m, Tel: 605-882-5200, Nearest town: Watertown. GPS: 44.894276, -97.242579

31 • C1 | Angostura SRA - Cascade

Total sites: 64, RV sites: 64, Elec sites: 64, Central water, Flush toilet, Free showers, RV dump, Tent & RV camping: $26, Also cabins, Plus $8 daily entrance fee, Open all year, Reservations accepted, Elev: 3218ft/981m, Tel: 605-745-6996, Nearest town: Hot Springs. GPS: 43.319121, -103.411268

32 • C1 | Angostura SRA - Cheyenne

Total sites: 22, RV sites: 22, Elec sites: 16, Central water, Flush toilet, Free showers, RV dump, Tents: $22/RVs: $26, Also cabins, Plus $8 daily entrance fee, Open all year, Reservations accepted, Elev: 3278ft/999m, Tel: 605-745-6996, Nearest town: Hot Springs. GPS: 43.339519, -103.414145

33 • C1 | Angostura SRA - Hat Creek

Total sites: 23, RV sites: 23, Elec sites: 23, Central water, Flush toilet, Free showers, No RV dump, Tent & RV camping: $26, Also cabins, Plus $8 daily entrance fee, Open all year, Reservations accepted, Elev: 3218ft/981m, Tel: 605-745-6996, Nearest town: Hot Springs. GPS: 43.301428, -103.400167

34 • C1 | Angostura SRA - Horsehead

Total sites: 51, RV sites: 51, Elec sites: 51, Central water, Flush toilet, Free showers, No RV dump, Tent & RV camping: $26, Also cabins, Plus $8 daily entrance fee, Open all year, Reservations accepted, Elev: 3225ft/983m, Tel: 605-745-6996, Nearest town: Hot Springs. GPS: 43.298111, -103.392657

35 • C1 | Angostura SRA - Sheps Canyon Horse Camp

Total sites: 11, RV sites: 11, Central water, Vault/pit toilet, No showers, No RV dump, Tent & RV camping: $26, Plus $8 daily entrance fee, Reservations accepted, Elev: 3199ft/975m, Tel: 605-745-6996, Nearest town: Hot Springs. GPS: 43.296975, -103.454004

36 • C1 | Angostura SRA Primitive

Dispersed sites, No water, Vault/pit toilet, Tent & RV camping: Free, Plus $8 daily entrance fee, Open all year, Elev: 3203ft/976m, Tel: 605-745-6996, Nearest town: Hot Springs. GPS: 43.297481, -103.446518

37 • C1 | Sheps Canyon Rec Area

Total sites: 22, RV sites: 22, Elec sites: 22, Central water, No toilets, No showers, No RV dump, Tent & RV camping: $26, Plus $8 daily entrance fee, Reservations accepted, Elev: 3202ft/976m, Tel: 605-745-6996, Nearest town: Hot Springs. GPS: 43.325295, -103.445989

38 • C3 | West Bend SRA

Total sites: 127, RV sites: 127, Elec sites: 114, Central water, Flush toilet, Free showers, RV dump, Tents: $19/RVs: $19-23, Also cabins, Plus $8 daily entrance fee, Open all year, Reservations accepted, Elev: 1427ft/435m, Tel: 605-773-2885, Nearest town: Pierre. GPS: 44.172173, -99.719428

39 • C4 | Burke Lake SRA

Total sites: 15, RV sites: 15, Central water, Vault/pit toilet, No showers, No RV dump, Tent & RV camping: $11, Plus $8 daily entrance fee, Open all year, Reservations not accepted, Elev: 2100ft/640m, Tel: 605-337-2587, Nearest town: Burke. GPS: 43.178957, -99.260116

40 • C4 | Buryanek SRA

Total sites: 44, RV sites: 44, Elec sites: 44, Central water, Flush toilet, Free showers, RV dump, Tent & RV camping: $23, Also cabins, Plus $8 daily entrance fee, Open all year, Reservations accepted, Elev: 1345ft/410m, Tel: 605-337-2587, Nearest town: Platte. GPS: 43.416669, -99.168723

41 • C4 | Platte Creek SRA - North CG

Total sites: 36, RV sites: 36, Elec sites: 24, Central water, Flush toilet, Free showers, RV dump, Tents: $16/RVs: $16-20, Plus $8 daily entrance fee, Open all year, Reservations accepted, Elev: 1417ft/432m, Tel: 605-337-2587, Nearest town: Platte. GPS: 43.300555, -99.001752

42 • C4 | Snake Creek SRA - North CG

Total sites: 97, RV sites: 97, Elec sites: 97, Central water, Flush toilet, Free showers, RV dump, Tent & RV camping: $26, Also cabins, Plus $8 daily entrance fee, Open all year, Reservations accepted, Elev: 1408ft/429m, Tel: 605-337-2587, Nearest town: Platte. GPS: 43.389059, -99.118485

43 • C4 | Snake Creek SRA - South CG

Total sites: 27, RV sites: 27, Elec sites: 27, Central water, Flush toilet, Free showers, RV dump, Tent & RV camping: $26, Also cabins, Plus $8 daily entrance fee, Open all year, Reservations accepted, Elev: 1414ft/431m, Tel: 605-337-2587, Nearest town: Platte. GPS: 43.385972, -99.111861

44 • C5 | Big Sioux SRA

Total sites: 49, RV sites: 43, Elec sites: 43, Water available, Flush toilet, Free showers, RV dump, Tents: $22/RVs: $26, Also cabins, Plus $8 daily entrance fee, Open all year, Reservations accepted, Elev: 1299ft/396m, Tel: 605-582-7243, Nearest town: Brandon. GPS: 43.575058, -96.598564

45 • C5 | Lake Vermillion SRA - East CG

Total sites: 37, RV sites: 37, Elec sites: 37, Central water, Vault/pit toilet, No showers, No RV dump, Tent & RV camping: $26, Also cabins, Plus $8 daily entrance fee, Open all year, Reservations accepted, Elev: 1444ft/440m, Tel: 605-296-3643, Nearest town: Sioux Falls. GPS: 43.599774, -97.167096

46 • C5 | Lake Vermillion SRA - North/West CG's

Total sites: 57, RV sites: 53, Elec sites: 53, Water available, Flush toilet, Free showers, RV dump, Tents: $22/RVs: $26, Plus $8 daily entrance fee, Open all year, Reservations accepted, Elev: 1470ft/448m, Tel: 605-296-3643, Nearest town: Sioux Falls. GPS: 43.593757, -97.181903

47 • C5 | Walker's Point SRA

Total sites: 43, RV sites: 42, Elec sites: 42, Central water, Flush toilet, Free showers, RV dump, Tents: $22/RVs: $22-26, Also cabins, Plus $8 daily entrance fee, Open all year, Reservations accepted, Elev: 1594ft/486m, Tel: 605-256-5003, Nearest town: Madison. GPS: 43.954627, -97.024694

48 • D4 | North Point SRA

Total sites: 115, RV sites: 115, Elec sites: 115, Central water, Flush toilet, Free showers, RV dump, Tent & RV camping: $26, Plus $8 daily entrance fee, Open all year, Reservations accepted, Elev: 1391ft/424m, Tel: 605-487-7046, Nearest town: Pickstown. GPS: 43.078872, -98.568184

49 • D4 | North Wheeler SRA

Total sites: 25, RV sites: 25, Elec sites: 25, Central water, Vault/pit toilet, No showers, No RV dump, Tents: $11/RVs: $11-15, Plus $8 daily entrance fee, Open all year, Reservations not accepted, Elev: 1401ft/427m, Tel: 605-487-7046, Nearest town: Platte. GPS: 43.167594, -98.822574

50 • D4 | Pease Creek SRA - Horse Camp

Total sites: 5, RV sites: 5, Central water, Vault/pit toilet, No showers, No RV dump, Tent & RV camping: $22, Plus $8 daily entrance fee, Open all year, Reservations accepted, Elev: 1457ft/444m, Tel: 605-487-7046, Nearest town: Geddes. GPS: 43.137909, -98.733532

51 • D4 | Pease Creek SRA - Main

Total sites: 23, RV sites: 23, Elec sites: 23, Central water, Flush toilet, Free showers, No RV dump, Tent & RV camping: $26, Plus $8 daily entrance fee, Open all year, Reservations accepted, Elev: 1453ft/443m, Tel: 605-487-7046, Nearest town: Geddes. GPS: 43.141836, -98.733964

52 • D4 | Randall Creek SRA

Total sites: 132, RV sites: 132, Elec sites: 132, Central water, Flush toilet, Free showers, RV dump, Tent & RV camping: $23, Also cabins, Open Mar-Nov, Reservations accepted, Elev: 1260ft/384m, Tel: 605-487-7046, Nearest town: Pickstown. GPS: 43.045635, -98.540726

53 • D4 | Springfield SRA

Total sites: 20, RV sites: 20, Elec sites: 19, Flush toilet, Free showers, RV dump, Tents: $19/RVs: $23, Plus $8 daily entrance fee, Open all year, Reservations accepted, Elev: 1237ft/377m, Tel: 605-668-2985, Nearest town: Springfield. GPS: 42.860176, -97.882258

54 • D5 | Chief White Crane SRA

Total sites: 146, RV sites: 146, Elec sites: 146, Water available, Flush toilet, Free showers, RV dump, Tent & RV camping: $26, Also cabins, Plus $8 daily entrance fee, Open all year, Reservations accepted, Elev: 1214ft/370m, Tel: 605-668-2985, Nearest town: Yankton. GPS: 42.852919, -97.460667

55 • D5 | Lewis and Clark SRA - East Midway

Total sites: 133, RV sites: 133, Elec sites: 133, Central water, Flush toilet, Free showers, RV dump, Tent & RV camping: $26, Plus $8 daily entrance fee, Open all year, Reservations accepted, Elev: 1243ft/379m, Tel: 605-668-2985, Nearest town: Yankton. GPS: 42.867779, -97.516708

56 • D5 | Lewis and Clark SRA - Gavins Point

Total sites: 90, RV sites: 90, Elec sites: 90, Central water, Flush toilet, Free showers, RV dump, Tent & RV camping: $26, Plus $8 daily entrance fee, Open all year, Reservations accepted, Elev: 1237ft/377m, Tel: 605-668-2985, Nearest town: Yankton. GPS: 42.860555, -97.536807

57 • D5 | Lewis and Clark SRA - Horse Camp

Total sites: 8, RV sites: 8, Elec sites: 8, Central water, Flush toilet, Free showers, RV dump, Tent & RV camping: $26, Plus $8 daily entrance fee, Open all year, Reservations accepted, Elev: 1253ft/382m, Tel: 605-668-2985, Nearest town: Yankton. GPS: 42.861568, -97.554382

58 • D5 | Lewis and Clark SRA - West Midway

Total sites: 68, RV sites: 68, Elec sites: 68, Central water, Flush toilet, Free showers, RV dump, Tent & RV camping: $26, Plus $8 daily entrance fee, Open all year, Reservations accepted, Elev: 1253ft/382m, Tel: 605-668-2985, Nearest town: Yankton. GPS: 42.864645, -97.526888

59 • D5 | Lewis and Clark SRA - Yankton

Total sites: 144, RV sites: 144, Elec sites: 144, Central water, Flush toilet, Free showers, RV dump, Tent & RV camping: $26, Same-day reservations only, $20 entrance fee for 1-7 days, Open all year,

Reservations accepted, Elev: 1230ft/375m, Tel: 605-668-2985, Nearest town: Yankton. GPS: 42.869041, -97.511239

60 • D5 | Pierson Ranch SRA

Total sites: 67, RV sites: 67, Elec sites: 67, Central water, Flush toilet, Free showers, RV dump, Tent & RV camping: $26, Also cabins, Plus $8 daily entrance fee, Open all year, Reservations accepted, Elev: 1214ft/370m, Tel: 605-668-2985, Nearest town: Yankton. GPS: 42.872939, -97.482532

Virginia

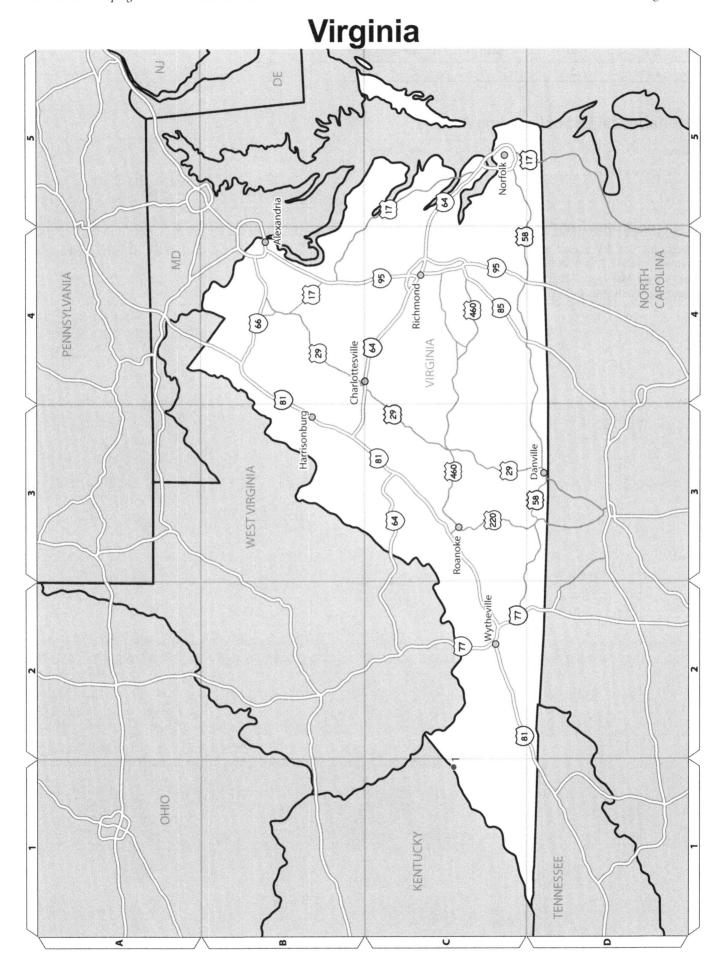

Map	ID	Map	ID
C1	1		

Alphabetical List of Camping Areas

Name   **ID**   **Map**

1 • C1 | Breaks Interstate Park

Total sites: 138, RV sites: 138, Elec sites: 115, Water at site, RV dump, Tents: $17/RVs: $24-26, Some Full hookups, $5 transaction fee, Open Mar-Nov, Elev: 1844ft/562m, Tel: 276-865-4413, Nearest town: Breaks. GPS: 37.290283, -82.294922

Washington

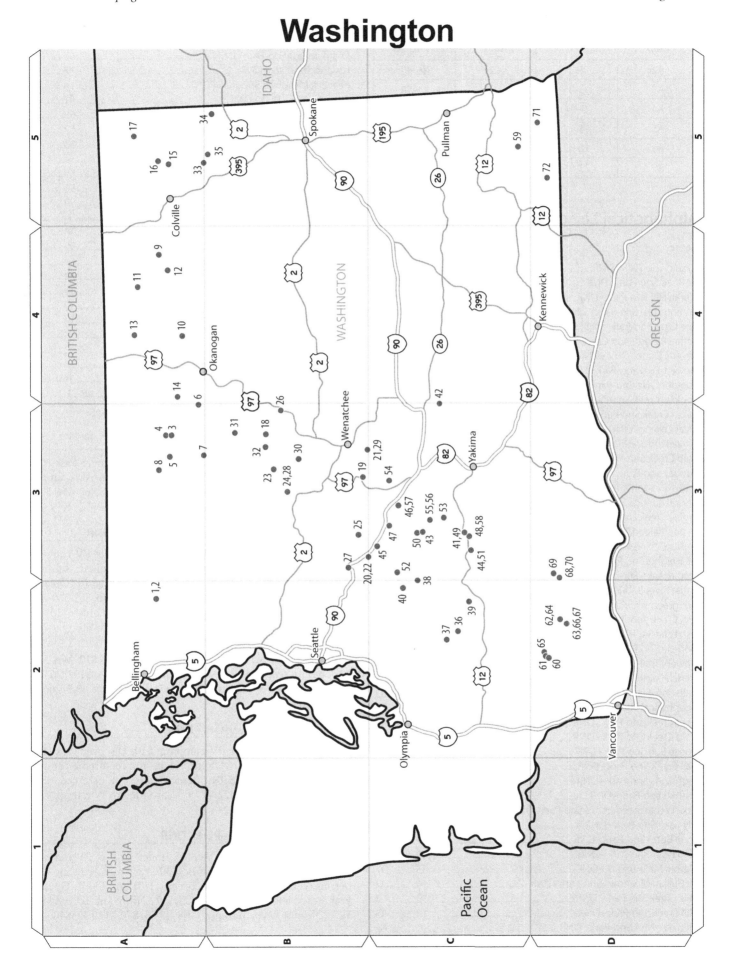

Map	ID	Map	ID
A2	1-2	C2	36-40
A3	3-8	C3	41-58
A4	9-14	C5	59
A5	15-17	D2	60-67
B3	18-32	D3	68-70
B5	33-35	D5	71-72

Alphabetical List of Camping Areas

Name	ID	Map
1 Road Sno-Park - DNR	36	C2
92 Road Sno-Park - DNR	37	C2
Albian Hill Sno-Park - DNR	9	A4
Antilon Lake Sno-Park - DNR	18	B3
Ape Cave Sno-Park - DNR	60	D2
Bethel Ridge/Soup Creek Sno-Park - DNR	41	C3
Beverly Dunes OHV - DNR	42	C3
Blewett Pass Sno-Park - DNR	19	B3
Boulder Cave Sno-Park - DNR	43	C3
Boulder Creek Sno-Park - DNR	3	A3
Cabin Creek Sno-Park - DNR	20	B3
Clear Lake Sno-Park - DNR	21	B3
Cloverland Sno-Park - DNR	71	D5
Cold Creek Sno-Park - DNR	44	C3
Cougar Sno-Park	61	D2
Crawfish Sno-Park - DNR	10	A4
Crystal Springs Sno-Park - DNR	22	B3
Curley Creek Sno-Park - DNR	62	D2
Easton Reload Sno-Park - DNR	45	C3
Eightmile Sno-Park - DNR	4	A3
Elk Heights Sno-Park - DNR	46	C3
Empire Lake Sno-Park - DNR	11	A4
Entiat River Sno-Park - DNR	23	B3
Evergreen Sno-Park - DNR	47	C3
Fish Creek Sno-Park - DNR	48	C3
Fish Lake Sno-Park - DNR	24	B3
Flodelle Sno-Park - DNR	15	A5
Flowery Trail Sno-Park - DNR	33	B5
French Cabin Sno-Park - DNR	25	B3
Gallagher Flat Wildlife Rec Area	26	B3
Geophysical Sno-Park - DNR	34	B5
Goat Creek Sno-Park - DNR	5	A3
Gold Creek Sno-Park - DNR	27	B3
Goose Egg Sno-Park - DNR	49	C3
Hall Creek Sno-Park - DNR	12	A4
Highlands Sno-Park - DNR	13	A4
Koshko Sno-Park - DNR	63	D2
Lake Wenatchee Airstrip Sno-Park - DNR	28	B3
Lily Lake Sno-Park - DNR	29	B3
Lone Butte Sno-Park - DNR	64	D2
Mad River Sno-Park - DNR	30	B3
Marble Mt Sno-Park - DNR	65	D2
McClellan Meadows Sno-Park - DNR	66	D2
Milk Creek Sno-Park - DNR	50	C3
Mill Creek Sno-Park - DNR	16	A5
Mt Baker NRA Sno-Park - DNR	1	A2
Ninebark Sno-Park - DNR	35	B5

North Summit Sno-Park - DNR	6	A3
Oldman Pass Sno-Park - DNR	67	D2
Paupac Sno-Park - DNR	17	A5
Peacock Meadows Sno-Park - DNR	14	A4
Pinegrass Sno-Park - DNR	51	C3
Pineside Sno-Park - DNR	68	D3
Pyramid Creek Sno-Park - DNR	52	C3
Rattlesnake Sno-Park - DNR	53	C3
Reecer Creek Sno-Park - DNR	54	C3
Rock Creek Lower Sno-Park - DNR	55	C3
Rock Creek Upper Sno-Park - DNR	56	C3
Rose Springs Sno-Park - DNR	59	C5
Shadows of the Sentinel Sno-Park - DNR	2	A2
Silver Springs Sno-Park - DNR	38	C2
Skate Creek Sno-Park - DNR	39	C2
Smith Butte Sno-Park - DNR	69	D3
Snow King Sno-Park - DNR	70	D3
South Fork Gold Creek Sno-Park - DNR	31	B3
Sun Top Sno-Park - DNR	40	C2
Taneum Sno-Park - DNR	57	C3
Tieton Airstrip Sno-Park - DNR	58	C3
Touchet Corral Sno-Park - DNR	72	D5
Twentyfive Mile Creek Sno-Park - DNR	32	B3
Twisp River Sno-Park - DNR	7	A3
Yellowjacket Sno-Park - DNR	8	A3

1 • A2 | Mt Baker NRA Sno-Park - DNR

Dispersed sites, Tent & RV camping: $10, Discover Pass ($10/day or $30/year) required, Sno-Park permit required if camping between 11/01 and 05/01, Elev: 1716ft/523m, Tel: 360-856-5700, Nearest town: Concrete. GPS: 48.675024, -121.740852

2 • A2 | Shadows of the Sentinel Sno-Park - DNR

Dispersed sites, No water, Vault/pit toilet, Tent & RV camping: $10, Discover Pass ($10/day or $30/year) required, Sno-Park permit required if camping between 11/01 and 05/01, Open all year, Reservations not accepted, Elev: 1002ft/305m, Tel: 360-856-5700, Nearest town: Concrete. GPS: 48.669433, -121.716113

3 • A3 | Boulder Creek Sno-Park - DNR

Dispersed sites, No toilets, Tent & RV camping: $10, WA Sno-Park permit required Nov-Mar, Open all year, Elev: 2103ft/641m, Tel: 509-422-7275, Nearest town: Winthrop. GPS: 48.572661, -120.170763

4 • A3 | Eightmile Sno-Park - DNR

Dispersed sites, Tent & RV camping: $10, Discover Pass ($10/day or $30/year) required, Sno-Park permit required if camping between 11/01 and 05/01, Reservations not accepted, Elev: 2126ft/648m, Tel: 509-422-7275, Nearest town: Winthrop. GPS: 48.599834, -120.167131

5 • A3 | Goat Creek Sno-Park - DNR

Dispersed sites, No water, Vault/pit toilet, Tent & RV camping: $10, Discover Pass ($10/day or $30/year) required, Sno-Park permit required if camping between 11/01 and 05/01, Open all year, Reservations not accepted, Elev: 2274ft/693m, Tel: 509-422-7275, Nearest town: Mazama. GPS: 48.581890, -120.373840

6 • A3 | North Summit Sno-Park - DNR

Dispersed sites, No water, Vault/pit toilet, Tent & RV camping: $10, Discover Pass ($10/day or $30/year) required, Sno-Park permit required if camping between 11/01 and 05/01, Open all year, Reservations not accepted, Elev: 4075ft/1242m, Tel: 509-422-7275, Nearest town: Twisp. GPS: 48.390536, -119.888820

7 • A3 | Twisp River Sno-Park - DNR

Dispersed sites, Tent & RV camping: $10, Discover Pass ($10/day or $30/year) required, Sno-Park permit required if camping between 11/01 and 05/01, Reservations not accepted, Elev: 2369ft/722m, Tel: 509-422-7275, Nearest town: Twisp. GPS: 48.359325, -120.353692

8 • A3 | Yellowjacket Sno-Park - DNR

Dispersed sites, No water, Vault/pit toilet, Tent & RV camping: $10, Discover Pass ($10/day or $30/year) required, Sno-Park permit required if camping between 11/01 and 05/01, Open all year, Reservations not accepted, Elev: 2415ft/736m, Tel: 509-422-7275, Nearest town: Mazama. GPS: 48.651447, -120.498924

9 • A4 | Albian Hill Sno-Park - DNR

Dispersed sites, No tents/RVs: Fee unk, Discover Pass ($10/day or $30/year) required, Sno-Park permit required if camping between 11/01 and 4/30, Elev: 4370ft/1332m, Tel: 509-684-7000, Nearest town: Republic. GPS: 48.632723, -118.445136

10 • A4 | Crawfish Sno-Park - DNR

Dispersed sites, No water, Vault/pit toilet, Tent & RV camping: $10, Discover Pass ($10/day or $30/year) required, Sno-Park permit required if camping between 11/01 and 05/01, Open all year, Elev: 4590ft/1399m, Tel: 509-422-7275, Nearest town: Riverside. GPS: 48.489072, -119.220781

11 • A4 | Empire Lake Sno-Park - DNR

Dispersed sites, No water, Vault/pit toilet, Tent & RV camping: Free, Discover Pass ($10/day or $30/year) required, Sno-Park permit required if camping between 11/01 and 05/01, Open all year, Elev: 3173ft/967m, Tel: 509-684-7000, Nearest town: Republic. GPS: 48.770303, -118.741105

12 • A4 | Hall Creek Sno-Park - DNR

Dispersed sites, No water, Vault/pit toilet, Tent & RV camping: $10, Discover Pass ($10/day or $30/year) required, Sno-Park permit required if camping between 11/01 and 05/01, Open all year, Elev: 3674ft/1120m, Tel: 509-684-7000, Nearest town: Republic. GPS: 48.575163, -118.586609

13 • A4 | Highlands Sno-Park - DNR

Dispersed sites, No water, Vault/pit toilet, Tent & RV camping: $10, Discover Pass ($10/day or $30/year) required, Sno-Park permit required if camping between 11/01 and 05/01, Open all year, Reservations not accepted, Elev: 3877ft/1182m, Tel: 509-486-2186, Nearest town: Tonasket. GPS: 48.803728, -119.205583

14 • A4 | Peacock Meadows Sno-Park - DNR

Dispersed sites, No water, Vault/pit toilet, Tent & RV camping: $10, Discover Pass ($10/day or $30/year) required, Sno-Park permit required if camping between 11/01 and 05/01, Open all year, Elev: 2608ft/795m, Tel: 509-422-7275, Nearest town: Conconully. GPS: 48.529295, -119.788937

15 • A5 | Flodelle Sno-Park - DNR

Dispersed sites, No water, Vault/pit toilet, Tent & RV camping: $10, Discover Pass ($10/day or $30/year) required, Sno-Park permit required if camping between 11/01 and 05/01, Reservations not accepted, Elev: 3114ft/949m, Tel: 509-382-4334. GPS: 48.546359, -117.578557

16 • A5 | Mill Creek Sno-Park - DNR

Dispersed sites, No tents/RVs: $10, Discover Pass ($10/day or $30/year) required, Sno-Park permit required if camping between 11/01 and 05/01, Reservations not accepted, Elev: 3222ft/982m, Tel: 509-684-7000, Nearest town: Colville. GPS: 48.611199, -117.551725

17 • A5 | Paupac Sno-Park - DNR

Dispersed sites, No water, Tent & RV camping: $10, Discover Pass ($10/day or $30/year) required, Sno-Park permit required if camping between 11/01 and 05/01, Reservations not accepted, Elev: 2822ft/860m, Tel: 509-684-7000, Nearest town: Ione. GPS: 48.765356, -117.296471

18 • B3 | Antilon Lake Sno-Park - DNR

Dispersed sites, No water, Vault/pit toilet, Tent & RV camping: $10, Discover Pass ($10/day or $30/year) required, Sno-Park permit required if camping between 11/01 and 05/01, Elev: 2300ft/701m, Tel: 509-663-9911, Nearest town: Chelan. GPS: 47.957864, -120.148990

19 • B3 | Blewett Pass Sno-Park - DNR

Dispersed sites, No water, Vault/pit toilet, Tent & RV camping: $10, Discover Pass ($10/day or $30/year) required, Sno-Park permit required if camping between 11/01 and 05/01, Open all year, Elev: 4265ft/1300m, Tel: 509-852-1100, Nearest town: Leavenworth. GPS: 47.332518, -120.578654

20 • B3 | Cabin Creek Sno-Park - DNR

Dispersed sites, No water, Vault/pit toilet, Tent & RV camping: $10, Discover Pass ($10/day or $30/year) required, Sno-Park permit required if camping between 11/01 and 05/01, Open all year, Reservations not accepted, Elev: 2479ft/756m, Tel: 509-852-1100, Nearest town: Leavenworth. GPS: 47.296609, -121.288686

21 • B3 | Clear Lake Sno-Park - DNR

Dispersed sites, No water, Vault/pit toilet, Tent & RV camping: $10, Discover Pass ($10/day or $30/year) required, Sno-Park permit required if camping between 11/01 and 05/01, Open all year, Elev: 2982ft/909m, Tel: 509-782-3065, Nearest town: Wenatchee. GPS: 47.296747, -120.300112

22 • B3 | Crystal Springs Sno-Park - DNR

Dispersed sites, No tents/RVs: $10, Discover Pass ($10/day or $30/year) required, Sno-Park permit required if camping between 11/01 and 05/01, Reservations not accepted, Elev: 2444ft/745m, Tel: 509-852-1100, Nearest town: Cle Elum. GPS: 47.305128, -121.319635

23 • B3 | Entiat River Sno-Park - DNR

Dispersed sites, No tents/RVs: $10, Discover Pass ($10/day or $30/year) required, Sno-Park permit required if camping between 11/01 and 05/01, Reservations not accepted, Elev: 1955ft/596m, Tel: 509-784-1511, Nearest town: Wenatchee. GPS: 47.909774, -120.485635

24 • B3 | Fish Lake Sno-Park - DNR

Dispersed sites, No water, Vault/pit toilet, Tent & RV camping: $10, Discover Pass ($10/day or $30/year) required, Sno-Park permit required if camping between 11/01 and 05/01, Open all year, Elev: 2021ft/616m, Tel: 509-548-6977, Nearest town: Leavenworth. GPS: 47.831875, -120.698058

25 • B3 | French Cabin Sno-Park - DNR

Dispersed sites, Tent & RV camping: $10, Discover Pass ($10/day or $30/year) required, Sno-Park permit required if camping between 11/01 and 05/01, Reservations not accepted, Elev: 2293ft/699m, Tel: 509-852-1100, Nearest town: Cle Elum. GPS: 47.356460, -121.109195

26 • B3 | Gallagher Flat Wildlife Rec Area

Dispersed sites, No water, No toilets, Tent & RV camping: Free, Elev: 719ft/219m, Nearest town: Chelan. GPS: 47.855822, -119.943358

27 • B3 | Gold Creek Sno-Park - DNR

Dispersed sites, No tents/RVs: $10, Discover Pass ($10/day or $30/year) required, Sno-Park permit required if camping between 11/01 and 05/01, Elev: 2861ft/872m, Tel: 509-852-1100, Nearest town: Snoqualmie Summit. GPS: 47.409294, -121.409808

28 • B3 | Lake Wenatchee Airstrip Sno-Park - DNR

Dispersed sites, No water, Vault/pit toilet, Tent & RV camping: $10, Discover Pass ($10/day or $30/year) required, Sno-Park permit required if camping between 11/01 and 05/01, Open all year, Reservations not accepted, Elev: 1975ft/602m, Tel: 509-548-6977, Nearest town: Leavenworth. GPS: 47.815949, -120.726342

29 • B3 | Lily Lake Sno-Park - DNR

Dispersed sites, No water, Vault/pit toilet, Tent & RV camping: $10, Discover Pass ($10/day or $30/year) required, Sno-Park permit required if camping between 11/01 and 05/01, Open all year, Elev: 2917ft/889m, Tel: 509-782-3065, Nearest town: Wenatchee. GPS: 47.302389, -120.308892

30 • B3 | Mad River Sno-Park - DNR

Dispersed sites, No water, No tents/RVs: $10, Discover Pass ($10/day or $30/year) required, Sno-Park permit required if camping between 11/01 and 05/01, Reservations not accepted, Elev: 1591ft/485m, Tel: 509-784-1511, Nearest town: Ardenvoir. GPS: 47.748765, -120.393539

31 • B3 | South Fork Gold Creek Sno-Park - DNR

Dispersed sites, No tents/RVs: $10, Discover Pass ($10/day or $30/year) required, Sno-Park permit required if camping between 11/01 and 05/01, Reservations not accepted, Elev: 2178ft/664m, Tel: 509-682-4900, Nearest town: Twisp. GPS: 48.156547, -120.150123

32 • B3 | Twentyfive Mile Creek Sno-Park - DNR

Dispersed sites, No tents/RVs: $10, Discover Pass ($10/day or $30/year) required, Sno-Park permit required if camping between 11/01 and 05/01, Reservations not accepted, Elev: 1824ft/556m, Tel: 509-682-4900, Nearest town: Chelan. GPS: 47.962466, -120.290353

33 • B5 | Flowery Trail Sno-Park - DNR

Dispersed sites, No water, No toilets, No tents/RVs: $10, Discover Pass ($10/day or $30/year) required, Sno-Park permit required if camping between 11/01 and 05/01, Reservations not accepted, Elev: 3976ft/1212m, Tel: 509-684-7000, Nearest town: Chewelah. GPS: 48.308649, -117.575729

34 • B5 | Geophysical Sno-Park - DNR

Dispersed sites, No water, Vault/pit toilet, Tent & RV camping: $10, Discover Pass ($10/day or $30/year) required, Sno-Park permit required if camping between 11/01 and 05/01, Open all year, Reservations not accepted, Elev: 2491ft/759m, Tel: 509-447-3129, Nearest town: Newport. GPS: 48.253922, -117.121195

35 • B5 | Ninebark Sno-Park - DNR

Dispersed sites, No tents/RVs: $10, Discover Pass ($10/day or $30/year) required, Sno-Park permit required if camping between 11/01 and 05/01, Elev: 3107ft/947m, Tel: 509-684-7000, Nearest town: Chewelah. GPS: 48.289037, -117.500365

36 • C2 | 1 Road Sno-Park - DNR

Dispersed sites, No water, Vault/pit toilet, Tent & RV camping: $10, Reservations not accepted, Elev: 6353ft/1936m, Nearest town: Ashford. GPS: 46.706074, -121.993176

37 • C2 | 92 Road Sno-Park - DNR

Dispersed sites, No water, Vault/pit toilet, Tent & RV camping: $10, Reservations not accepted, Elev: 2305ft/703m, Nearest town: Elbe. GPS: 46.781829, -122.080389

38 • C2 | Silver Springs Sno-Park - DNR

Dispersed sites, No water, Vault/pit toilet, Tent & RV camping: $10, Discover Pass ($10/day or $30/year) required, Sno-Park permit required if camping between 11/01 and 05/01, Open all year, Reservations not accepted, Elev: 2751ft/839m, Tel: 509-653-1400, Nearest town: Greenwater. GPS: 46.978933, -121.534561

39 • C2 | Skate Creek Sno-Park - DNR

Dispersed sites, No tents/RVs: $10, Discover Pass ($10/day or $30/year) required, Sno-Park permit required if camping between 11/01 and 05/01, Reservations not accepted, Elev: 1841ft/561m, Tel: 360-497-1100, Nearest town: Packwood. GPS: 46.638333, -121.711687

40 • C2 | Sun Top Sno-Park - DNR

Dispersed sites, No water, Vault/pit toilet, Tent & RV camping: $10, Discover Pass ($10/day or $30/year) required, Sno-Park permit required if camping between 11/01 and 05/01, Open all year, Reservations not accepted, Elev: 2240ft/683m, Tel: 509-653-1400, Nearest town: Greenwater. GPS: 47.067558, -121.594106

41 • C3 | Bethel Ridge/Soup Creek Sno-Park - DNR

Dispersed sites, No water, No toilets, No tents/RVs: $10, Discover

Pass ($10/day or $30/year) required, Sno-Park permit required if camping between 11/01 and 05/01, Reservations not accepted, Elev: 2674ft/815m, Tel: 509-653-1400, Nearest town: Naches. GPS: 46.673137, -121.088274

42 • C3 | Beverly Dunes OHV - DNR

Total sites: 8, RV sites: 8, No water, Vault/pit toilet, Tent & RV camping: $10, No fires, Discover Pass ($10/day or $30/year) required, Elev: 503ft/153m, Tel: 509-925-0973, Nearest town: Beverly. GPS: 46.829152, -119.894606

43 • C3 | Boulder Cave Sno-Park - DNR

Dispersed sites, No tents/RVs: $10, Discover Pass ($10/day or $30/year) required, Sno-Park permit required if camping between 11/01 and 05/01, Reservations not accepted, Elev: 2484ft/757m, Tel: 509-653-1400. GPS: 46.951948, -121.079783

44 • C3 | Cold Creek Sno-Park - DNR

Dispersed sites, No tents/RVs: $10, Discover Pass ($10/day or $30/year) required, Sno-Park permit required if camping between 11/01 and 05/01, Reservations not accepted, Elev: 3351ft/1021m, Tel: 509-653-1400, Nearest town: Naches. GPS: 46.626896, -121.255685

45 • C3 | Easton Reload Sno-Park - DNR

Dispersed sites, No water, Vault/pit toilet, Tent & RV camping: $10, Winter camping only, Sno-Park permit required if camping between 11/01 and 05/01, Open all year, Reservations not accepted, Elev: 2270ft/692m, Tel: 509-852-1100. GPS: 47.235441, -121.223362

46 • C3 | Elk Heights Sno-Park - DNR

Dispersed sites, Tent & RV camping: $10, Discover Pass ($10/day or $30/year) required, Sno-Park permit required if camping between 11/01 and 05/01, Reservations not accepted, Elev: 2342ft/714m, Tel: 509-852-1100, Nearest town: Cle Elum. GPS: 47.100922, -120.786265

47 • C3 | Evergreen Sno-Park - DNR

Dispersed sites, No tents/RVs: $10, Discover Pass ($10/day or $30/year) required, Sno-Park permit required if camping between 11/01 and 05/01, Elev: 2287ft/697m, Tel: 509-852-1100, Nearest town: Cle Elum. GPS: 47.156377, -121.025042

48 • C3 | Fish Creek Sno-Park - DNR

Dispersed sites, No water, Vault/pit toilet, Tent & RV camping: $10, Discover Pass ($10/day or $30/year) required, Sno-Park permit required if camping between 11/01 and 05/01, Reservations not accepted, Elev: 2953ft/900m, Tel: 509-653-1400, Nearest town: Naches. GPS: 46.627018, -121.131535

49 • C3 | Goose Egg Sno-Park - DNR

Dispersed sites, No water, Vault/pit toilet, Tent & RV camping: $10, Discover Pass ($10/day or $30/year) required, Sno-Park permit required if camping between 11/01 and 05/01, Open all year, Reservations not accepted, Elev: 2564ft/782m, Tel: 509-653-1400, Nearest town: Naches. GPS: 46.667938, -121.089048

50 • C3 | Milk Creek Sno-Park - DNR

Dispersed sites, No tents/RVs: $10, Discover Pass ($10/day or $30/year) required, Sno-Park permit required if camping between 11/01 and 05/01, Reservations not accepted, Elev: 2576ft/785m, Tel: 509-684-7000, Nearest town: Naches. GPS: 46.982041, -121.093620

51 • C3 | Pinegrass Sno-Park - DNR

Dispersed sites, Vault/pit toilet, Tent & RV camping: $10, Discover Pass ($10/day or $30/year) required, Sno-Park permit required if camping between 11/01 and 05/01, Reservations not accepted, Elev: 3409ft/1039m, Tel: 509-653-1400, Nearest town: Naches. GPS: 46.623108, -121.260478

52 • C3 | Pyramid Creek Sno-Park - DNR

Dispersed sites, No water, No toilets, No tents/RVs: $10, Discover Pass ($10/day or $30/year) required, Sno-Park permit required if camping between 11/01 and 05/01, Reservations not accepted, Elev: 2716ft/828m, Tel: 360-825-6585, Nearest town: Greenwater. GPS: 47.113425, -121.457688

53 • C3 | Rattlesnake Sno-Park - DNR

Dispersed sites, No water, No toilets, No tents/RVs: $10, Discover Pass ($10/day or $30/year) required, Sno-Park permit required if camping between 11/01 and 05/01, Reservations not accepted, Elev: 2139ft/652m, Tel: 509-653-1400, Nearest town: Naches. GPS: 46.811319, -120.947828

54 • C3 | Reecer Creek Sno-Park - DNR

Dispersed sites, No water, No toilets, No tents/RVs: $10, Discover Pass ($10/day or $30/year) required, Sno-Park permit required if camping between 11/01 and 05/01, Elev: 2805ft/855m, Tel: 509-852-1100, Nearest town: Ellensburg. GPS: 47.160352, -120.613404

55 • C3 | Rock Creek Lower Sno-Park - DNR

Dispersed sites, No water, Vault/pit toilet, No tents/RVs: $10, Discover Pass ($10/day or $30/year) required, Sno-Park permit required if camping between 11/01 and 05/01, Reservations not accepted, Elev: 2474ft/754m, Tel: 509-653-1400, Nearest town: Naches. GPS: 46.893268, -120.968934

56 • C3 | Rock Creek Upper Sno-Park - DNR

Dispersed sites, No water, Vault/pit toilet, No tents/RVs: $10, Discover Pass ($10/day or $30/year) required, Sno-Park permit required if camping between 11/01 and 05/01, Reservations not accepted, Elev: 3432ft/1046m, Tel: 509-653-1400, Nearest town: Naches. GPS: 46.906921, -120.966423

57 • C3 | Taneum Sno-Park - DNR

Dispersed sites, Tent & RV camping: $10, Discover Pass ($10/day or $30/year) required, Sno-Park permit required if camping between 11/01 and 05/01, Reservations not accepted, Elev: 2493ft/760m, Tel: 509-852-1100, Nearest town: Cle Elum. GPS: 47.106396, -120.853967

58 • C3 | Tieton Airstrip Sno-Park - DNR

Dispersed sites, No water, Vault/pit toilet, No tents/RVs: $10, Discover Pass ($10/day or $30/year) required, Sno-Park permit required if camping between 11/01 and 05/01, Reservations not accepted, Elev: 2930ft/893m, Tel: 509-653-1400, Nearest town: Rimrock. GPS: 46.638994, -121.124013

59 • C5 | Rose Springs Sno-Park - DNR

Dispersed sites, No tents/RVs: $10, Discover Pass ($10/day or $30/year) required, Sno-Park permit required if camping between 11/01 and 05/01, Reservations not accepted, Elev: 4770ft/1454m, Tel: 509-843-1891, Nearest town: Pomeroy. GPS: 46.275843, -117.557058

60 • D2 | Ape Cave Sno-Park - DNR

Dispersed sites, No water, Vault/pit toilet, Tent & RV camping: $10, Discover Pass ($10/day or $30/year) required, Sno-Park permit required if camping between 11/01 and 05/01, Open all year, Reservations not accepted, Elev: 1899ft/579m, Tel: 360-449-7800, Nearest town: Cougar. GPS: 46.099349, -122.212993

61 • D2 | Cougar Sno-Park

Dispersed sites, No tents/RVs: Fee unk, Discover Pass ($10/day or $30/year) required, Sno-Park permit required if camping between 11/01 and 05/01, Elev: 2165ft/660m, Tel: 360-449-7800, Nearest town: Cougar. GPS: 46.119855, -122.206766

62 • D2 | Curley Creek Sno-Park - DNR

Dispersed sites, No tents/RVs: Fee unk, Discover Pass ($10/day or $30/year) required, Sno-Park permit required if camping between 11/01 and 05/01, Elev: 2959ft/902m, Tel: 509-395-3400, Nearest town: Carson. GPS: 46.026672, -121.891069

63 • D2 | Koshko Sno-Park - DNR

Dispersed sites, No water, Vault/pit toilet, No tents/RVs: $10, Discover Pass ($10/day or $30/year) required, Sno-Park permit required if camping between 11/01 and 05/01, Elev: 2979ft/908m, Tel: 509-395-3400, Nearest town: Carson. GPS: 45.998177, -121.913512

64 • D2 | Lone Butte Sno-Park - DNR

Dispersed sites, No tents/RVs: $10, Discover Pass ($10/day or $30/year) required, Sno-Park permit required if camping between 11/01 and 05/01, Reservations not accepted, Elev: 3199ft/975m, Tel: 509-395-3400, Nearest town: Carson. GPS: 46.044027, -121.859373

65 • D2 | Marble Mt Sno-Park - DNR

Dispersed sites, No tents/RVs: $10, Discover Pass ($10/day or $30/year) required, Sno-Park permit required if camping between 11/01 and 05/01, Elev: 2697ft/822m, Tel: 360-449-7800, Nearest town: Cougar. GPS: 46.129895, -122.171363

66 • D2 | McClellan Meadows Sno-Park - DNR

Dispersed sites, No water, No tents/RVs: $10, Discover Pass ($10/day or $30/year) required, Sno-Park permit required if camping between 11/01 and 05/01, Elev: 2943ft/897m, Tel: 509-395-3400, Nearest town: Carson. GPS: 46.009355, -121.901713

67 • D2 | Oldman Pass Sno-Park - DNR

Dispersed sites, No tents/RVs: $10, Discover Pass ($10/day or $30/year) required, Sno-Park permit required if camping between 11/01 and 05/01, Elev: 3077ft/938m, Tel: 509-395-3400, Nearest town: Carson. GPS: 45.990225, -121.913215

68 • D3 | Pineside Sno-Park - DNR

Dispersed sites, No water, Vault/pit toilet, Tent & RV camping: $10, Sno-Park permit required if camping between 11/01 and 05/01, Open all year, Reservations not accepted, Elev: 2776ft/846m, Tel: 509-395-3400, Nearest town: Carson. GPS: 46.048985, -121.500931

69 • D3 | Smith Butte Sno-Park - DNR

Dispersed sites, No tents/RVs: $10, Discover Pass ($10/day or $30/year) required, Sno-Park permit required if camping between 11/01 and 05/01, Elev: 3908ft/1191m, Tel: 509-395-3400, Nearest town: Trout Lake. GPS: 46.078954, -121.453646

70 • D3 | Snow King Sno-Park - DNR

Dispersed sites, No tents/RVs: $10, Discover Pass ($10/day or $30/year) required, Sno-Park permit required if camping between 11/01 and 05/01, Elev: 3310ft/1009m, Tel: 509-395-3400, Nearest town: Trout Lake. GPS: 46.054565, -121.471953

71 • D5 | Cloverland Sno-Park - DNR

Dispersed sites, No tents/RVs: $10, Discover Pass ($10/day or $30/year) required, Sno-Park permit required if camping between 11/01 and 05/01, Reservations not accepted, Elev: 4738ft/1444m, Tel: 509-843-1891, Nearest town: Asotin. GPS: 46.148217, -117.335207

72 • D5 | Touchet Corral Sno-Park - DNR

Dispersed sites, No tents/RVs: $10, Discover Pass ($10/day or $30/year) required, Sno-Park permit required if camping between 11/01 and 05/01, Elev: 4291ft/1308m, Tel: 509-382-4334, Nearest town: Dayton. GPS: 46.093647, -117.847604

Wisconsin

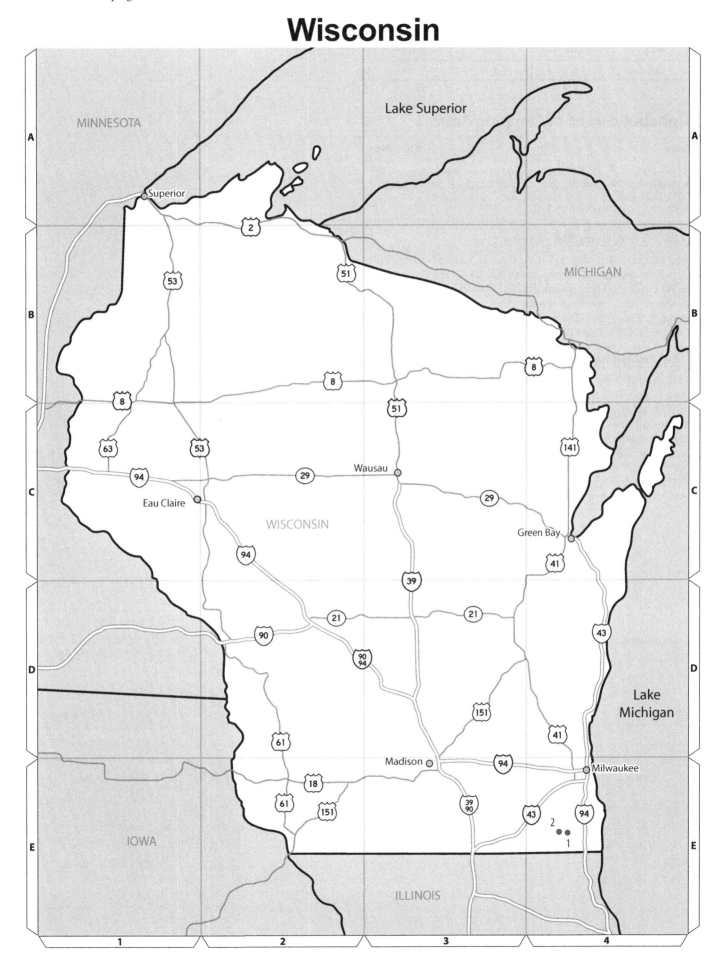

Map	ID	Map	ID
E4	1-2		

Alphabetical List of Camping Areas

Name **ID** **Map**

1 • E4 | Richard Bong SRA - Sunrise

Total sites: 117, RV sites: 117, Elec sites: 54, Central water, Flush toilet, Free showers, RV dump, Tents: $20-23/RVs: $33-35, $5 off for WI residents, Daily entrance fee $11 ($8 WI residents), Lower off-season rates, Stay limit: 14 days, Open all year, Reservations accepted, Elev: 834ft/254m, Tel: 262-878-5600, Nearest town: Kansasville. GPS: 42.633397, -88.115089

2 • E4 | Richard Bong SRA - Sunset

Total sites: 98, RV sites: 98, Elec sites: 1, Central water, Flush toilet, Free showers, RV dump, Tents: $20-23/RVs: $33-35, $5 off for WI residents, Daily entrance fee $11 ($8 WI residents), Lower off-season rates, Stay limit: 14 days, Open all year, Reservations accepted, Elev: 813ft/248m, Tel: 262-878-5600, Nearest town: Kansasville. GPS: 42.633904, -88.185162

Wyoming

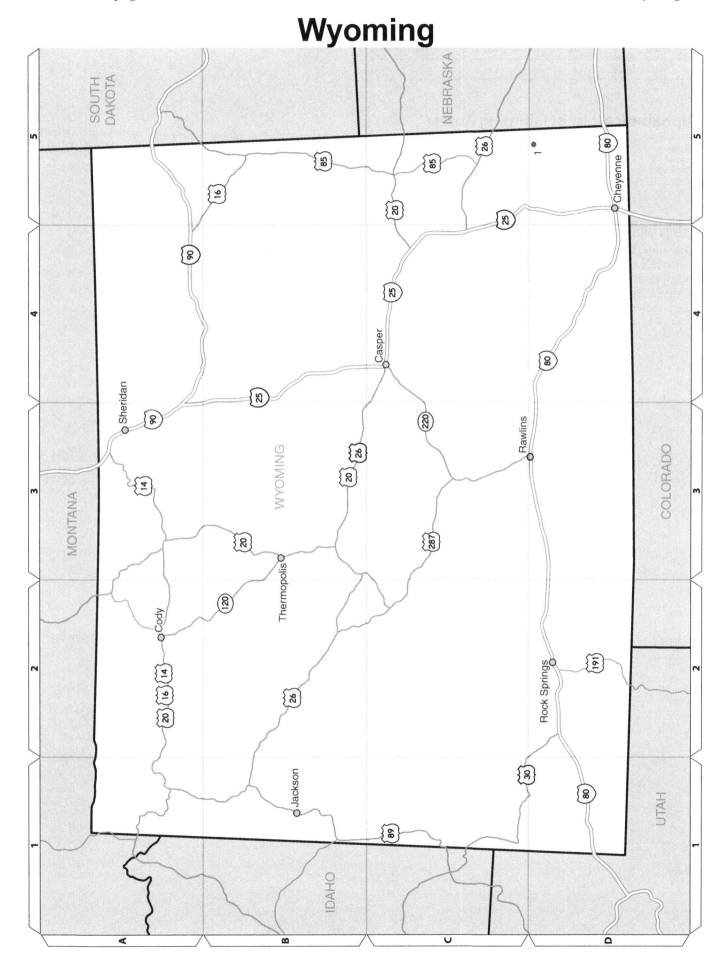

Map	ID	Map	ID
D5	1		

Alphabetical List of Camping Areas

Name   **ID**   **Map**

Hawk Springs SRA .... 1 .... D5

1 • D5 | Hawk Springs SRA

Total sites: 24, RV sites: 24, Central water, Vault/pit toilet, No showers, No RV dump, Tent & RV camping: $10-18, No water in winter, Daily use fee:$7-$12, Lower use & camp fees are for WY residents, Open all year, Elev: 4508ft/1374m, Tel: 307-836-2334, Nearest town: Guernsey. GPS: 41.708957, -104.193338

Made in the USA
Las Vegas, NV
10 August 2024

93620642R00057